impact

WORKBOOK 3

SERIES EDITORS
JoAnn (Jodi) Crandall
Joan Kang Shin

NATIONAL GEOGRAPHIC LEARNING

Australia • Brazil • Mexico • Singapore • United Kingdom • United States

Unit 1

Who Am I?

1 **Unscramble these words that describe personality.** Complete the sentence under the picture with one of the words.

1. sienthaustic enthusiastic
2. engeretic ______
3. regesonu ______
4. otimpicsit ______
5. nopsibleres ______
6. asmbiouti ______
7. ermindeted ______
8. goutinog ______
9. itpante ______
10. gasidoren ______
11. fidconent ______
12. bborstun ______

Look at his desk!
He's so ______.

2 **Write.** Complete each sentence with a word from Activity 1.

1. She believes that good things will happen. She's optimistic.
2. They won't allow anyone or anything to stop them. They're ______.
3. Janet makes friends easily. She's ______.
4. He shows great passion for cooking. He's ______.
5. You can trust him to take care of things. He's ______.
6. Mario worked hard. He's ______ he will do well in his final exams.
7. You are always very calm. You're so ______.
8. She does a lot of things in one day! She's ______.
9. Gina is so ______. She never listens to anyone's advice.
10. She wants to be successful and famous. She's ______.
11. They are very kind and share what they have. They're ______.

3 **Listen.** Complete the dialogue with the missing words. Then listen again to check your answers. In class, take turns reading the dialogue with a classmate. 002

Lucy: Sorry I couldn't go to the cinema with you. I had to look after my little brother, Mike.

Sam: I look after my little brother sometimes. But it's like Tommy isn't even there. He's very quiet and not too ________________ .

Lucy: You're lucky. Unlike Tommy, Mike is loud and noisy. He's always running through the house. He's too ________________ . And he's so messy. He's not ________________ at all.

Sam: Tommy isn't that way at all. He isn't as ________________ as Mike. He likes to read, play video games and draw.

Lucy: Well, they're alike in that they are both ________________ about video games.

Sam: I love video games, just like they do. Don't you?

Lucy: Not me!

4 **Write.** List four words that describe your personality. Write a sentence about your personality for each word.

shy	I find it difficult to talk to people because I'm shy.
1. ________________	________________
	________________
2. ________________	________________
	________________
3. ________________	________________
	________________
4. ________________	________________
	________________

GRAMMAR

Question tags: Confirming information or seeking agreement

Cookery programmes **are** competitive, **aren't they**?	**Yes**, **they are**. My friends love them.
They **couldn't** go on holiday, **could they**?	**No**, their flight was cancelled.
Tom **didn't** like the party, **did he**?	**No, he didn't.** He is too shy.
Carla and Luke **will** help me prepare dinner, **won't they**?	**No, they won't.** They're not very enthusiastic about cooking.

Question tags are short questions at the end of statements. A positive statement has a negative tag. The expected answer is positive. A negative statement has a positive tag. The expected answer is negative.

A listener can disagree or answer differently to what's expected. In this case, there is often some explanation.

1 **Listen.** Circle the correct tag. Then listen and check your answers. 003

1. Jack Andraka's idea won at the competition, **didn't he** / **(didn't it)**?
2. Sugar on cauliflower is odd, **isn't it** / **aren't they** ?
3. You have to be ambitious to do well, **don't you** / **haven't you** ?
4. Children shouldn't ride bicycles without helmets, **don't they** / **should they** ?
5. Your mum can speak three languages, **doesn't she** / **can't she** ?
6. Young people won't spend time cooking, **will they** / **don't they** ?
7. Fast food is good for you, **isn't it** / **doesn't it** ?
8. He couldn't find all the ingredients, **didn't he** / **could he** ?

2 **Match each response with the correct question in Activity 1.** Write the number of the question on the line. Then listen again and check your answers. 004

__5__ a. No, she can only speak two.

_____ b. Yes, it's very strange!

_____ c. No, he couldn't. It's a shame.

_____ d. Yes, it did. He's going to be on TV.

_____ e. Yes, it's important if you want to do well.

_____ f. No, it isn't. It's not healthy.

_____ g. No, it's dangerous!

_____ h. No. They like spending their time with friends.

3 **Read.** Complete each sentence with a word from the box. Then add a question tag.

competitive	confident	co-operative	helpful	jealous	open-minded	outgoing

1. Lisa doesn't like working in groups. She isn't very ______________, ________?
2. Athletes focus a lot on their training and diet so they can be the best. They can be very ______________, ________?
3. Children are stubborn and don't listen to suggestions. They won't always be ______________, ________?
4. Tim is very funny but he's also shy. He should be more ______________, ________?
5. Mr Larkins knows where to find interesting information. He could be very ______________, ________?
6. The players weren't ______________ that they would win, ________?

4 **Write.** Answer the questions and give additional information.

1. You live very near your school, don't you?
   Yes, I do. I live just ten minutes away.
2. You haven't been to Italy, have you?
   ____
3. You would like to be a scientist, wouldn't you?
   ____
4. You're an only child, aren't you?
   ____
5. You didn't play any sports last week, did you?
   ____

1 **Listen and read.** As you read the article, notice the descriptive words and expressions that describe an only child. 005

SUPER FIRSTBORNS

What makes us who we are? Is it the environment we grow up in? Is it the people we live with? Some experts tell us that half of our personality is genetics – our natural make-up, or the way we are born. Gender – whether you're a boy or a girl – is also a consideration. Age is another factor. In families with more than one child, birth order is sometimes thought to be important. But some families have only one child.

Another name for only children is 'onlies', though experts sometimes refer to an only child as a 'super firstborn'. This is because an only child has many of the advantages of the firstborn child but doesn't experience the changes of a new baby arriving in the family. There is no competition from a sibling – a brother or sister – so onlies have their parents' full attention. Some onlies are mature and responsible because they spend a lot of time with adults. They learn to be self-entertainers and can be creative and imaginative when the adults around them are busy.

On the other hand, some only children can become jealous of their parents' adult friends. They can be self-centred and selfish if these friends ignore them and take too much attention away from them. They may be used to feeling important and can appear spoilt when things don't go their way. Some onlies who aren't used to sharing can be bossy around other children.

What happens when there is only a birth order of one? As we've seen, birth order is just one of many factors that can influence our personalities and affect the way we are.

2 **Look for words and phrases that describe an only child in the article.** List them in one of the categories.

Positive Qualities	Negative Qualities
mature	jealous

3 **Read and answer the questions.**

1. Why are only children referred to as 'super firstborns'?

____

2. Why can only children sometimes be more imaginative?

____

3. Why do some onlies find it difficult to play with other children?

____

4 **Read 'Super Firstborns' again.** Complete the idea web with factors that influence personality. Can you think of any other factors to add? Write them on the lines.

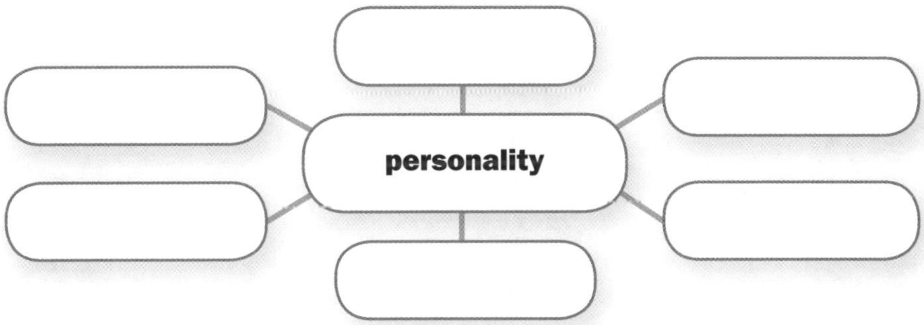

____________________ ____________________

5 **In your own words, describe two of the factors that you feel most influenced you.**

____

____

____

GRAMMAR

Using *it* to talk about weather, time and distance, and for emphasis

It's a sunny day. Let's go out.	**It**'s great that she won.
It's 11 o'clock at night. **It**'s time to go home.	**It** upsets me when my brother is bossy.
It's the 22nd today. **It**'s my birthday!	I love **it** when she smiles.
It was five miles to Robert's house.	I don't like **it** when I'm late for class.

We use ***it*** to talk about the weather and to express time, dates and distance. ***It*** does not refer to any specific person, thing or place. ***It*** is the subject of the sentence.

We also use ***it*** to introduce a sentence that expresses an opinion or to provide emphasis. (In '*It*'s great that she won', ***it*** has the same meaning as the words *that she won*.)

1 **Listen.** Write the number of the sentence you hear next to the correct picture. 006

a. ______

b. ______

c. ______

d. ______

e. ______

f. ______

2 **Complete the sentences with your own ideas.**

1. It annoys me when ______________________________.
2. It's great that ______________________________.
3. It's weird that ______________________________.
4. It's not fair that ______________________________.
5. It makes me happy when ______________________________.

3 **Read.** Circle the uses of *it*. Then answer the questions using *it*.

It's my birthday tomorrow and I don't know what to do!

I looked at the weather forecast for tomorrow and it will be cold and windy on the beach. I hate it when it's too cold on the beach; you can't go for a swim.

My friends and I could go to my favourite restaurant. But it would take 45 minutes to get there.

Or, we could go to the cinema. There's a popular film I'd like to see. But it's Friday and I can't buy the tickets today. Then tomorrow the cinema will be crowded and we won't be able to get tickets.

It's a shame that I can't have a party at home. My mum and dad hate it when there is a mess and a lot of noise.

It just drives me crazy when I can't decide what to do!

1. What day of the week is Tanya's birthday?

___

2. Why doesn't Tanya want to go to the beach?

___

3. Why doesn't she want to go to her favourite restaurant?

___

4. Why can't she go to the cinema?

___

5. Why can't she have a party at home?

___

WRITING

We use certain expressions when we want to **compare** (write about similarities) or **contrast** (write about differences). We use words such as the following examples to compare or contrast two people, places or things.

- *Compare*: alike both in the same way too
- *Contrast*: although but on the other hand unlike

1 Organise.

1. Your task is to compare and contrast your personality with that of a family member or friend. Think about how you are similar to and different from the person you chose. Make notes in the Venn diagram about your personalities and also about your hobbies and interests.

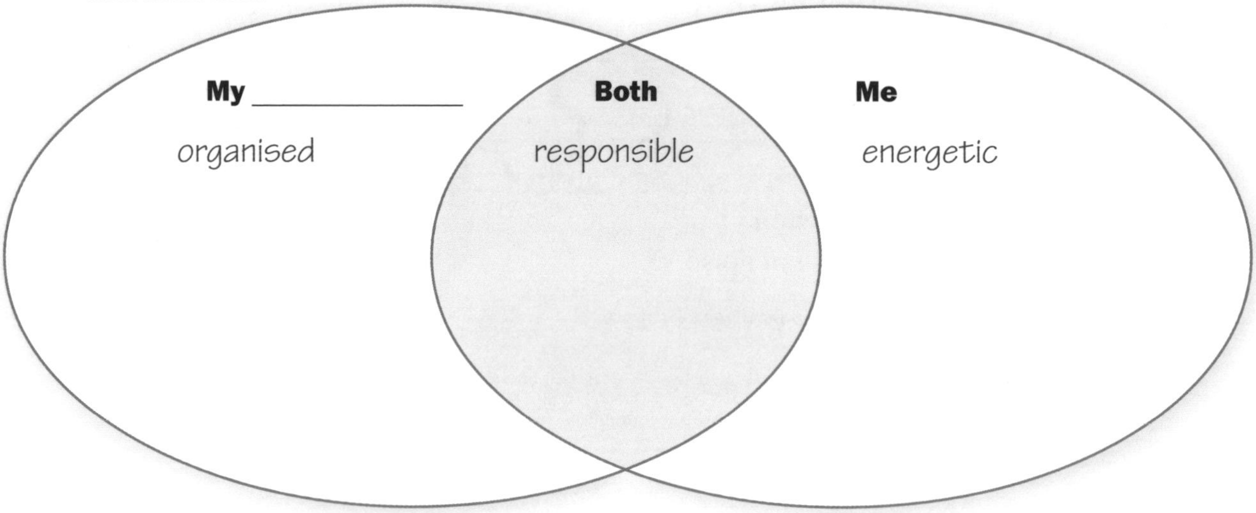

2. Think about how you will introduce your family member or friend. Write a possible topic sentence here.

____

Next, you'll need a paragraph describing how you and your family member or friend are similar and a paragraph about how you're different. Use the words from the Writing box.

Finally, write a concluding paragraph saying whether you and your family member or friend are more similar than different, or more different than similar.

2 Write.

1. Go to page 21 in your book. Re-read the model and writing prompt.
2. Write your first draft. Check for organisation, content, punctuation, capitalisation and spelling.
3. Check your final draft. Share it with your teacher and classmates.

Now I can ...

· talk about personality and character traits.

☐ Yes, I can!
☐ I think I can.
☐ I need more practice.

What three words describe you? I'm ____________________,
____________________ and ____________________.

What makes you special? I'm ____________________,
____________________ and ____________________.

· use question tags to confirm information or seek agreement.

☐ Yes, I can!
☐ I think I can.
☐ I need more practice.

Jack Andraka is an inventor, ____________________?

Brothers and sisters don't always agree, ____________________?

Only children can be more imaginative, ____________________?

· use *it* to talk about weather, time and distance and for emphasis.

☐ Yes, I can!
☐ I think I can.
☐ I need more practice.

Wednesday

____

five-thirty

____

raining

____

my birthday

____

· write about similarities and differences between two people.

☐ Yes, I can!
☐ I think I can.
☐ I need more practice.

Choose two of your friends and describe them. How are they similar? How are they different?

____

____

____

YOU DECIDE Choose an activity. Go to page 90.

Unit 2

Misunderstood Animals

1 **Play Bingo.** Use the words below to fill in the blank after each item. Cross out each word as you use it. Write a definition of the word that's left.

slimy	aggressive	crucial
ecosystem	pest	disgusting
poisonous	sting	filthy

1. Cross out the word that means very dirty. ____________________
2. Cross out the word that describes an animal that might attack you.

   ____
3. Cross out the word that describes a snail or a fish. ____________________
4. Cross out the word that means absolutely necessary. ____________________
5. Cross out the word that describes what a wasp will do if attacked.

   ____
6. Cross out the word for something that can cause sickness or death.

   ____
7. Cross out the word that means very unpleasant. ____________________
8. Cross out the word that describes everything that exists in a particular environment. ____________________

   The word that is left is ____________________.

   A ____________________ is ____________________

   ____.

2 **Read.** Circle the correct word to complete each statement.

1. **Pests** / **Bees** are beneficial to humans.
2. Some snakes are **filthy** / **poisonous**.
3. We **conserve** / **destroy** the environment when we cut down trees.
4. The rubbish smells terrible. It's **crucial** / **disgusting**.
5. Crocodiles can be **aggressive** / **crucial** if their babies are in danger.
6. Cities try to **control** / **decay** the number of pigeons living there.
7. **Stings** / **Germs** are all around us. We must try to be clean.
8. Cats and dogs are **popular** / **unpopular** pets in many places.

3 **Listen.** Then match the first part of each sentence with its ending. Write the letter on the line. 007

_____ 1. In some parts of India, snakes are valued

_____ 2. Pigmy rattlesnake venom is used

_____ 3. Experts use spider silk

_____ 4. Experts have copied sharkskin

_____ 5. Wasps play a crucial part in the ecosystem

_____ 6. Slimy snails are garden pests,

a. because they help farmers protect their crops from pests.

b. to make biodegradable bottles, bandages and bulletproof jackets.

c. to create a new heart medicine.

d. but birds and other animals like to eat them.

e. because they control the rat population.

f. and created a plastic that stops germs spreading in hospitals.

4 **Choose a misunderstood animal.** Write two interesting facts about it. Use words from the box.

aggressive	beneficial	crucial	ecosystem	germs	pest	poisonous	sting

____

____

____

GRAMMAR

Modals: Speculating about the past

Lorrie is afraid of the water. (fact)
She **could have fallen** into a swimming pool when she was a child. (not sure)
She **might have seen** a shark. (not sure)
She **may have been stung** by a jellyfish. (fairly sure)
She **must have had** a bad experience involving the water. (very sure)

We use ***could have***, ***might have***, ***may have***, ***must have*** + participle to show how sure or certain we are about past situations.

1 **Read and match.** There are two responses for each statement. Write the letters.

Statements

_____ 1. Eric came back from the jungle covered in red spots.

_____ 2. They decided never to go on safari again.

_____ 3. Maya changed her mind about becoming a zoologist.

_____ 4. The crowd looked scared.

_____ 5. Julia and Anna don't want to go into the water.

_____ 6. Jenny couldn't sleep last night.

Responses

a. They may have seen jellyfish.
b. She must have realised she'd have to experiment with animals.
c. They might have seen some vampire bats.
d. She might have heard wolves howling outside her window.
e. She may have seen a cockroach on her bedroom wall.
f. A tropical insect must have stung him.
g. They must have heard strange noises.
h. They must have encountered a dangerous animal.
i. They must have heard about the shark attack last week.
j. Mosquitoes may have bitten him.
k. She may have decided she'll make more money as a vet.
l. They may have seen lions killing another animal.

2 **Listen.** First, complete the sentences. Then, think about how certain the speaker is about the boy's situation. Write *not sure*, *fairly sure* or *very sure* on the line after each answer.

008

The boy was very upset when he came out of the cave.

1. He ____________________ scared of the dark. ____________________
2. He ____________________ into a spider's web. ____________________
3. He ____________________ and hurt himself. ____________________
4. He ____________________ the slimy cave walls. ____________________
5. He ____________________ the myth about the ____________________ poisonous cave snake.

3 **Complete.** Use the words from the box and *could have, may have, might have* or *must have* with the verb given in brackets.

beneficial	**bite**	**~~cockroach~~**	**decay**	**disgusting**	**slimy**	**upset**

1. She saw something run under the rubbish bin.

   She <u>could have seen</u> (see) a <u>cockroach</u>. (not sure)

2. He felt something ____________________ .

   He ____________________ (touch) a snail. (very sure)

3. The students said that the snake's ____________________ was poisonous.

   They ____________________ (misunderstand) the teacher. (fairly sure)

4. The kitten was getting ____________________ .

   It ____________________ (want) more milk. (not sure)

5. He thinks that bees are not ____________________ to people.

   He ____________________ (read) the wrong information. (fairly sure)

6. The rubbish smelt ____________________ .

   They ____________________ (forget) to collect it. (very sure)

1 **Listen and read.** As you read, notice the similarities between crocodiles and birds. 009

CROCODILES:

THE TRUTH EXPOSED

Crocodiles aren't slimy or poisonous. They don't sting or suck your blood like some insects do. They do have a lot of sharp teeth, but no poisonous fangs. So why are people scared of crocodiles? Well, crocodiles are very big and very strong. They have a reputation for being aggressive. They're not pleasant to look at and their scales are rough.

Although crocodiles are reptiles and may look like big lizards, they are in fact more closely related to birds. They also share some behaviours with birds. Like some birds, crocodiles guard their nests and protect their young for up to two years, until they're old enough to survive on their own. Some crocodiles actually hold the food in their mouths when they feed their young just like birds do.

Crocodiles are caring parents. Crocodile mums will carry their babies in their mouths to protect them from harm. They teach them to swim just like mother ducks teach their ducklings. If an adult crocodile believes that a baby croc is in danger, it will go to that baby to protect it, even if they are not related.

These images paint a different picture of crocodiles. What is more, some cultures actually value and respect them because they are believed to represent the spirit of ancestors. In Australia, where there is a huge population of saltwater crocodiles, people learn how to behave safely. For example, people don't go back repeatedly to the same place on riverbanks to wash their clothes. They know that crocodiles recognise patterns and routines.

Experts tell us that crocodiles are sensitive, clever and even emotional creatures. Their huge size and their teeth may be threatening, but it's a misconception that all crocodiles kill and eat people. Most crocodiles aren't aggressive towards people and, like snakes, will avoid human contact when they can.

2 **Read.** Tick **T** for *True* or **F** for *False*. Rewrite the false statements to make them true.

	T	F
1. Crocodiles are big and strong reptiles.	☐	☐
2. Crocodiles eat their babies.	☐	☐
3. Crocodiles look after their young.	☐	☐
4. Crocodiles help only their own young when they're in danger.	☐	☐
5. All crocodiles kill people.	☐	☐
6. Education is important in understanding crocodile behaviour.	☐	☐
7. Crocodiles are not intelligent animals.	☐	☐

____

____

____

____

3 **Complete the table with details about birds and crocodiles.** Use your own knowledge, information from the text or other sources.

	Appearance	Habitat	Behaviour
Birds	*beak*	*seashore*	*build nests*
Crocodiles			

4 **Answer the questions in your own words.**

1. What is one misconception you had about crocodiles?

____

2. What are some interesting facts you learnt about crocodiles? List at least two.

____

3. How can we change the way we think about crocodiles?

____

GRAMMAR

Infinitives with *to*	Infinitives without *to*
I like **to look** at insects. My brother hopes **to get** a snake for his birthday. That parrot is beginning **to annoy** me! Why did you agree **to take** care of Mica's rat? You don't like rats!	My mum won't let me **have** a pet spider. Please help your sister **feed** her rat. We will **visit** the spider sanctuary on Saturday. Every morning, we hear the birds **sing**.

We use the infinitive with ***to*** after some common verbs: *agree, ask, begin, decide, like, need, plan, want.*

There is no ***to*** after: modals (*can, will, might, could*), verbs describing the senses (*see, hear, feel*) and certain other verbs such as *let, watch* and *make.*

The verb *help* can be used with or without ***to***: *Can you help me **(to) feed** the spiders?*

1 **Read.** To complete each sentence, circle the verb with *to* or without *to.*

1. She felt something **crawl / to crawl** up her leg.
2. My brother made me **touch / to touch** a hairy spider!
3. We asked them **leave / to leave** their pet snake at home.
4. You might **want / to want** to see what your pet spider is eating!
5. Are you really planning **get / to get** a pet tarantula?

2 **Listen.** Complete the sentences with an infinitive with *to* or without *to.* 010

choose **eat** **get** **hope** **pack** ~~**take**~~

1. He's not planning ___to take___ his rat to the vet.
2. He didn't remember ________________ the mosquito net.
3. I didn't let my sister ________________ our pet snake.
4. She saw a spider ________________ a very big insect.
5. I want ________________ help to control my fear of spiders.

3 **Read the e-mail.** Add *to* where it is needed. If *to* is not needed, write *X*.

Dear Miyako,

Thank you for your interest in Big Heart Animal Rehabilitation Centre.

My name is Rebecca Nkosi and I'm in charge of the volunteer programme. Here's some information about what we do.

Every summer we recruit young volunteers __to__ come and work at our centre. We have many animals that we need ______ take care of. We try ______ rescue exotic pets that shouldn't ______ be pets in the first place!

People ask whether we can ______ return rescued animals to the wild. Unfortunately, we can't ______ let these animals ______ go back to the wild because they're too sick or weak and most were born in captivity. We use these animals ______ teach visitors about the difficulties they would ______ face in the wild. We want people ______ learn ______ choose the right pets!

We're looking for volunteers to help us ______ feed, clean and provide exercise for our animals. If you want ______ become a volunteer, visit our website and explain why you would like ______ join our team. We hope ______ hear from you soon!

Rebecca

4 **Write.** Why should Rebecca choose you? Complete the sentences and questions you might send to her.

1. I would love ______________________________.
2. I'm very good with animals. I learnt ______________________________.
3. I can ______________________________.
4. At the centre, will I ______________________________?
5. Would I need ______________________________?
6. I'm planning ______________________________.

WRITING

A process description explains a purpose through a sequence of steps in the order in which they happen.

Purpose: I went to the zoo	**in order to** control **so that** I could control	my fear of snakes.

Sequence:

Before *I went to the zoo, I was scared of snakes.* **During** *my visit, I became familiar with the snakes.* **After** *I left the zoo, I felt more comfortable about snakes.*

First, *I saw the snakes behind the glass.* **Then,** *I watched them as they moved around.* **Next,** *I held one for a few minutes.* **Finally,** *I relaxed!*

1 Organise.

1. Your task is to describe the process of training a pit bull puppy to help people better understand your dog. Find out about this breed of dog. Research what type of training you will need to do. Write the main ideas in the table below.

How to Train a Pit Bull Puppy

2. Look at your notes. Number the steps you would need to follow to train your dog.

   Think about the purpose of your description. Write a possible topic sentence to tell your reader the purpose of your description.

   ____

   Now write the different steps here:

   Step 1: ___________________________________

   Step 2: ___________________________________

   Step 3: ___________________________________

   Step 4: ___________________________________

   Finally, think about your expected results. This will be your summary.

2 Write.

1. Go to page 37 in your book. Re-read the model and the writing prompt.
2. Write your first draft. Check for organisation, punctuation, capitalisation and spelling.
3. Check your final draft. Share it with your teacher and classmates.

Now I can ...

- **talk about misunderstood animals and their role in the environment.**

☐ Yes, I can!
☐ I think I can.
☐ I need more practice.

Describe why or how snakes and vampire bats are misunderstood.

____

____

____

____

- **use modals to speculate about the past.**

☐ Yes, I can!
☐ I think I can.
☐ I need more practice.

Say what happened.

The children couldn't stop laughing! They ______________________.

She woke up very late. She ______________________.

- **use infinitives with *to* or without *to*.**

☐ Yes, I can!
☐ I think I can.
☐ I need more practice.

Finish the sentences.

I like ______________________.

My friend plans ______________________.

Our family will ______________________.

Let me ______________________.

- **write a process description showing purpose and sequence.**

☐ Yes, I can!
☐ I think I can.
☐ I need more practice.

Complete the sentences with sequencing words.

________, she told the dog to sit. ________, she gave the dog a reward. ______________ the dog understood that it would get a reward for good behaviour.

YOU DECIDE **Choose an activity.** Go to page 91.

Units 1–2 Review

1 **Read.** Then choose the correct word to complete each sentence.

1. When Marc decides he doesn't want to do something, he doesn't! He's so ____ .
   a. self-confident b. stubborn c. ambitious

2. Petra doesn't like speaking in front of the class, does she? She's too ____ .
   a. self-conscious b. self-confident c. outgoing

3. Clara's parents have always given her everything she asks for. She's very ____ .
   a. determined b. generous c. spoilt

4. Ben's dream is to sail alone around the world. He has spent the last three years training. He's also saving to buy a better boat. He's definitely ____ .
   a. determined b. organised c. fair

5. Gabi loves cooking. She invites friends to lunch every weekend so she can cook for them and try out new recipes. She's very ____ .
   a. co-operative b. competitive c. enthusiastic

2 **Read.** First, match each word with its definition. Then, use the words to complete the text about salamanders.

____	1. A strong and forceful way to do something		a. poison
____	2. A story told in ancient culture to explain a belief		b. misconception
____	3. So unpleasant that it makes you feel slightly ill		c. slimy
____	4. Everything that exists in a particular environment		d. ecosystem
____	5. Covered in a thick, slippery liquid		e. myth
____	6. Producing good or helpful results		f. disgusting
____	7. A wrong idea or belief		g. beneficial
____	8. A substance causing people to die or become very ill		h. aggressive

Salamanders have a moist ______________ body that we find ______________ to touch. Most salamanders produce a milky ______________ to protect themselves. They can also leave their tail behind to distract an ______________ predator. Fortunately, it only takes salamanders a few weeks to grow back lost tails. Scientists are investigating this ability to see how it might be ______________ to human medicine.

Long ago, people believed that salamanders were born from fire because they often crawled out quickly when a log was thrown on a fire. The ______________ that clothes made from salamander skin can protect you from fire is another ______________ .

Salamanders can live up to 20 years. However, changes in the ______________ are threatening their existence.

3 **Read.** Then choose the best answer to fill in each blank.

Have Pets Got Personalities?

We are all very different, (1) _____ ? No two people are exactly alike. No two humans have exactly the same personality, (2) _____ ?

Personality is something that we associate with human beings, but animals have personalities, too. Some pets make themselves at home very easily. We love (3) _____ when we find that our new pet has become another member of the family! Of course, we are very happy to let these animals (4) _____ be part of our lives.

It may be difficult to notice the personality of a goldfish, but cats and dogs certainly show you when they're happy, sad or upset. We can (5) _____ notice their body language: a wagging tail, an arched back or no eye contact. Some dogs can be very protective of their owners. If a dog doesn't stop barking, you know that something (6) _____ happened.

Scientists hope (7) _____ find out more about animal personalities so that they can identify a way to help people who are ill or are living on their own. Until then, be aware that your pet can be sensitive. If your goldfish is swimming around in circles, or your hamster is being aggressive, they (8) _____ had a bad day!

1.	a. isn't it	b. are we	c. aren't we	**5.**	a. to	b. it	c. –
2.	a. don't they	b. have they	c. haven't they	**6.**	a. must	b. must have	c. could
3.	a. it	b. one	c. to	**7.**	a. to	b. in	c. –
4.	a. –	b. to	c. they	**8.**	a. can have	b. may	c. might have

4 **Write.** Complete the last sentence in each item so that the meaning is the same as in the first sentence or sentences.

1. I become upset when I see another person cry.
   ________________________ me when I see another person cry.

2. We were worried at first. We thought someone had stolen her handbag.
   We thought that someone ________________________ her handbag.

3. It's true that you need to be ambitious to succeed.
   You have to be ambitious to succeed, ________________________ ?

4. She cooks amazing meals. I'm fairly sure she took a cookery course.
   She cooks amazing meals. She ________________________ a cookery course.

5. Their dream is to travel around the world.
   They ________________________ travel around the world.

6. The time has come for us to leave.
   ________________________ for us to leave.

Unit 3

Everybody's Doing It!

1 **Find nine more vocabulary words in the word search.** Look at the **bold** words in the reading on pages 44–45 of your book. You can look for words in any direction in the word search. The first one is done for you.

C	F	B	E	T	A	R	G	I	M	F	N
C	O	N	S	E	N	S	U	S	T	L	O
P	R	O	A	C	Q	E	S	G	K	E	U
E	M	D	R	J	U	W	D	U	N	A	X
Q	A	V	A	D	O	O	C	J	M	D	B
N	T	T	N	E	I	C	I	F	F	E	H
D	I	S	X	T	P	N	Y	B	L	R	R
W	O	L	L	A	H	E	A	O	H	I	E
F	N	R	A	C	S	R	N	T	Z	M	F
O	I	Z	U	K	M	G	R	K	E	P	E
S	W	E	G	P	C	N	W	M	L	D	R
B	K	Q	L	A	I	T	N	E	T	O	P

2 **Match some of the words from Activity 1 to the definitions.**

1. leader — A person who directs and leads others
2. ______ — Something that can become a real possibility
3. ______ — An agreement or opinion that everyone shares
4. ______ — To move from one place to another at different times of year
5. ______ — To think that something is true without really knowing
6. ______ — To be part of or be a member of a group or organisation
7. ______ — Working in a well-organised and productive way
8. ______ — Organised so that people work together efficiently and well

3 **Listen to the information about humpback whales.** Then read the sentences and tick **T** for *True* or **F** for *False*. 011

	T	F
1. Humpback whales have teeth.	☐	☐
2. Whales hunt in collective groups. Two whales attack while other whales wait and chase the fish.	☐	☐
3. Many whales migrate from colder waters to warmer waters.	☐	☐
4. Breaching is another name for whale migration.	☐	☐
5. Whales can communicate efficiently through songs.	☐	☐
6. Scientists still aren't sure if whale songs are meant to attract potential partners.	☐	☐

4 **Complete each sentence with a verb from the box.** Make any necessary changes so the verb's tense fits the sentence.

assemble	assume	belong	co-ordinate	lead	migrate	mimic	realise	remain

1. Fifty elephants ______________________ across the forest towards the east.
2. A bear usually ______________________ in its habitat and sleeps during the winter.
3. Stop ______________________ me! You're always copying me.
4. One goose ______________________ the others as they fly in a flock.
5. The crowd ______________________ outside the football stadium, ready to go in.
6. He ______________________ to the young explorers club. He goes there every Friday.
7. The owners ______________________ that their dog wouldn't attack the chickens. But they were wrong!
8. Next year, various wildlife organisations ______________________ activities to protect the Amazon rain forest.

GRAMMAR

Phrasal verbs

Separable	Inseparable
The scientists **handed in** *their report.*	They **thought about** *collective behaviour.*
The scientists **handed** *their report* **in.**	They **thought about** *it.*
The scientists **handed** *it* **in.**	We **looked at** *the migrating birds.*
	We **looked at** *them.*

Some phrasal verbs can be separated. Others cannot.

With **separable** phrasal verbs, the object can go either between the two parts or after:
They picked ***the rubbish*** *up.* OR *They picked up* ***the rubbish****.*

If the object is a pronoun, it must always come between the two parts: *They picked* ***it*** *up.*

With **inseparable** phrasal verbs, the *object* and *object pronoun* can only go after the two parts:
He flew over ***the rain forest****. He flew over* ***it****.*

1 Circle the word that completes each sentence.

1. The scientists wondered **about** / **with** the collective behaviour of the geese.
2. The children drew and cut **out** / **to** circular shapes.
3. The team worked **up** / **out** the answer and reached a consensus of what to do next.
4. The journalist asked the crowd to point **across** / **out** their leader.
5. I prefer to remain here and wait **for** / **at** the bus stop.
6. The teacher talked **with** / **about** a more efficient system of studying.

2 Listen. Write the sentences. Then underline the phrasal verbs and circle the objects. 012

1. Ants work the problem out together.
2. ______
3. ______
4. ______
5. ______
6. ______

3 **Choose three sentences from Activity 2.** Re-write them. First, move the position of the object. Then, replace the object with a pronoun.

1. Ants work out the problem together.

   Ants work it out together.

2. ______________________________

   ____

3. ______________________________

   ____

4. ______________________________

   ____

4 **Look at the pictures.** Then choose a phrasal verb to complete each sentence. Make any necessary changes.

1. 

2. 

3. 

4. 

5. 

come across	**look after**	**put on**	**talk about**	**wait for**	**wonder about**

1. Does a pack of wolves have a leader that ______________ the others?
2. The farmer ______________ a swarm of bees at the entrance to the field.
3. She watched and ______________ the flock of migrating birds.
4. They ______________ the herd of elephants to cross the road.
5. She ______________ the behaviour of a troop of gorillas.

1 Listen and read. As you read, notice how the word *example* is used. 013

Swarm robotics and microrobotics are a new type of technology. This technology has produced a new generation of robots whose design is directly influenced and inspired by nature. Experts have realised that there is a lot to learn from the animal kingdom's efficient system of co-operation.

Scientists studied the collective behaviour of ants. Ants join together to solve problems and they do this for the benefit of their community. Ants have been on the planet for much longer than humans and have had millions of years of practice living in large groups.

The interesting thing is that an ant doesn't stand out as an individual. It has poor eyesight and little ability to think on its own. Together, however, ants show off higher-order intelligence. This is also true of bees, flocks of birds and schools of fish.

Following examples from nature, robotics designers have tried to mimic collective and swarm behaviour. They've found ways to divide technology and capabilities among different robots. The intention is to build a group of robots that is able to swarm, or join together, to solve problems. One robot on its own won't be able to work out a problem, but it won't need to!

Swarm robotics has many potential uses. Robotic bees, for example, can help farmers with crop pollination. Flying robots can search through a building during disasters to look for and locate survivors. They have also been used to map the environment in Kenya. This has allowed environmentalists to observe the behaviour of animals such as baboons, and the impact of pests such as locusts, on vegetation for hundreds of miles.

Right now, teams of biologists, scientists and engineers are trying to work out how to make space and ocean floor exploration possible using this new technology. What's more, all this expert teamwork shows that, although insects have been co-operating for millions of years, humans can do it, too! Ants are an example to us all!

2 **Read the article in Activity 1 and then answer the questions.**

1. Highlight the word *example* in the text.
   a. Circle any use of *example* that means *a model that we should follow or imitate.*
   b. Underline any use of *example* that means *something that helps to explain or confirm that something is true.*
2. Underline the explanation of *collective behaviour* that is correct.
   a. A group of people, a crowd, a mob or a fashion trend.
   b. A group of people who spontaneously or in a temporary way respond to the same event or situation.
3. Choose the best explanation for the statement: 'One robot on its own won't be able to work out the problem.'
   a. A robot will need to work and collaborate with other robots to solve a problem.
   b. No robot will be able to understand the problem.

3 **In what areas can swarm robotics benefit us?** Complete the idea web. Write one idea in each circle. Then choose one of the areas. Write two sentences describing how swarm robotics actually benefits us in that area. Include some of your own ideas.

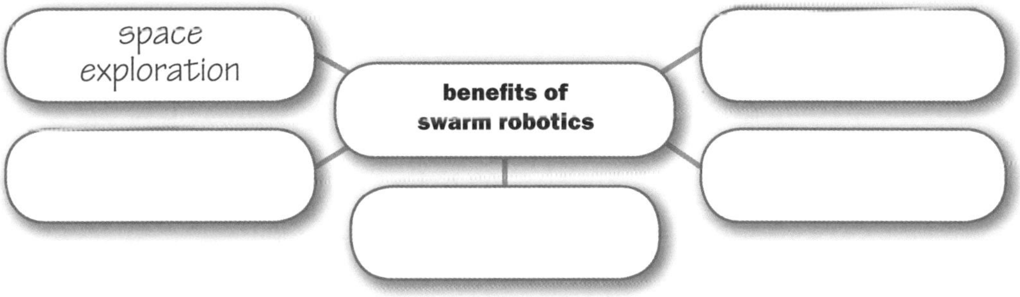

____

____

4 **The text suggests that humans can be good at working together the way ants and robots do.** List four ways you are co-operative and work well with others.

____

____

____

____

GRAMMAR

***Enough, too much, too many*: Talking about amount**

There are **not enough** *volunteer groups* to visit people in hospitals.
We have **enough** *music* for the party.
There were **too many** *people* at the concert. I couldn't dance!
You spend **too much** *time* on your own. Come and join us.

We use ***enough*** before uncountable nouns (nouns with no plural forms: *money, music, advice*) or plural countable nouns (*chairs*) to describe the right amount.

We use ***not enough*** before uncountable nouns (*time*) or plural countable nouns (*chairs*) to describe less than the amount needed.

We use ***too many*** before plural countable nouns (*bags*) and ***too much*** before uncountable nouns (*rubbish*) to describe that there is more of something than needed.

1 **Listen.** Circle the correct word. Complete the sentences with *enough, not enough, too much* or *too many.* 014

1. The neighbours were making ________________ **pasta** / **noise**.
2. We'll have ________________ **time** / **space** to join the flash mob if we hurry.
3. You won't sleep if you drink ________________ **coffee** / **tea**.
4. There were ________________ **security guards** / **people** outside the stadium.
5. There was ________________ **work** / **water** for the volunteers.
6. There was ________________ **light** / **time** to take a photo of the flock of birds.
7. ________________ **traffic** / **pollution** in our cities is not healthy.
8. My daughter spends ________________ **minutes** / **hours** on her mobile phone.

2 **Look back at Activity 1.** Write the number of the sentence next to the correct description to indicate its meaning.

a. Less than needed: __________

b. More than needed: __________

c. The right amount: __________

3 **Read the letter of complaint.** Underline the uses of *enough, too much* and *too many.* Then, complete the manager's reply using these words and the appropriate noun from the text.

Dear Sir/Madam,

I am writing to complain about what happened yesterday at your supermarket.

It started when I couldn't find a parking space. Normally, there are enough parking spaces, but yesterday the car park was full. I had to pay to leave my car on the street!

Next, when I tried to enter the supermarket, there were just too many people around the entrance. Because of the crowd, I couldn't get in for almost 15 minutes. When I finally got inside the shop, I saw that you were giving customers a free bar of chocolate.

I also saw that some people took too many bars. One lady, for example, took ten bars, and then five other people copied her! This sort of behaviour meant that there weren't enough chocolate bars for everybody. Obviously, if you want to do this type of activity, you should have enough staff to control the crowd.

I got the last bar but when I tried it, I found that it had too much sugar! At least I was able to do my shopping, but I didn't enjoy the experience.

Yours faithfully,

Mrs Ranier

Dear Mrs Ranier,

I'm sorry that you had a bad experience at our shop. I apologise that there weren't ________________________. We will refund what you paid on the street. I'm sorry that there were ________________________ outside and that it took you a long time to get into the shop. We'll try to do better next time, so this won't happen again. I realise that we didn't have ________________________ to control this type of group behaviour. We have apologised to all our customers because there weren't ________________________.

I'm sorry that you didn't like the chocolate because it had ________________________.

We hope that you come back to our shop and that your next visit will be more pleasant.

Kind regards,

The Management

WRITING

We use examples to explain and support the main idea of a piece of writing. We can introduce examples with the following phrases:

for example   for instance   in other words   such as

*Some pets, **such as** dogs and cats, like to mimic their owners. **In other words**, they copy their owners' behaviour. **For instance**, when I start singing, my dog starts howling! **In other words**, my dog likes to do the same things that I do.*

1 Organise.

1. Your topic is *Group Behaviour.* Choose a human or an animal group behaviour and write a description of it. Try to include several examples to explain and support your description. Look through the unit for ideas on human and animal group behaviour.

Group Behaviour:
Examples

2. Start by describing the context. (*Every Saturday I go to the shopping centre; In the afternoons, I take my dog out to the park; The other day I watched an interesting documentary on meerkats.*) Write your introductory sentence here:

____

____

Think about what phrases you will use to give examples of the group behaviour you observed or heard about. Can you use the phrase *in other words* to conclude or finish your description? Can you add another group behaviour you have observed that links to your previous description?

2 Write.

1. Go to page 55 in your book. Re-read the model and writing prompt.
2. Write your first draft. Check for organisation, content, punctuation, capitalisation and spelling.
3. Check your final draft. Share it with your teacher and classmates.

Now I can ...

· **talk about human and animal group behaviour.**

☐ Yes, I can!
☐ I think I can.
☐ I need more practice.

What's one reason you would join a group?

____

____

What are some advantages and disadvantages of animals being in groups?

____

____

· **use phrasal verbs.**

☐ Yes, I can!
☐ I think I can.
☐ I need more practice.

Choose one separable and one inseparable phrasal verb. Write two sentences with each. First, use an object and then replace it with an object pronoun.

1. ______________________________

____

2. ______________________________

____

· **use *enough, too much* and *too many* to talk about amounts.**

☐ Yes, I can!
☐ I think I can.
☐ I need more practice.

There were ______________ boats on the river. We couldn't move!

I took ______________ water to last me three days.

______________ sun isn't good for you. You can get burnt.

· **write a descriptive essay about a group behaviour.**

☐ Yes, I can!
☐ I think I can.
☐ I need more practice.

Underline the appropriate phrase to introduce an example.

Fish, *in other words* / *such as* tuna, swim in schools for protection.

Crowds at a football match or a concert, *for example* / *such as,* have no leaders.

YOU DECIDE Choose an activity. Go to page 92.

Unit 4

Fashion Footprints

1 **Read the clues.** Then complete the puzzle.

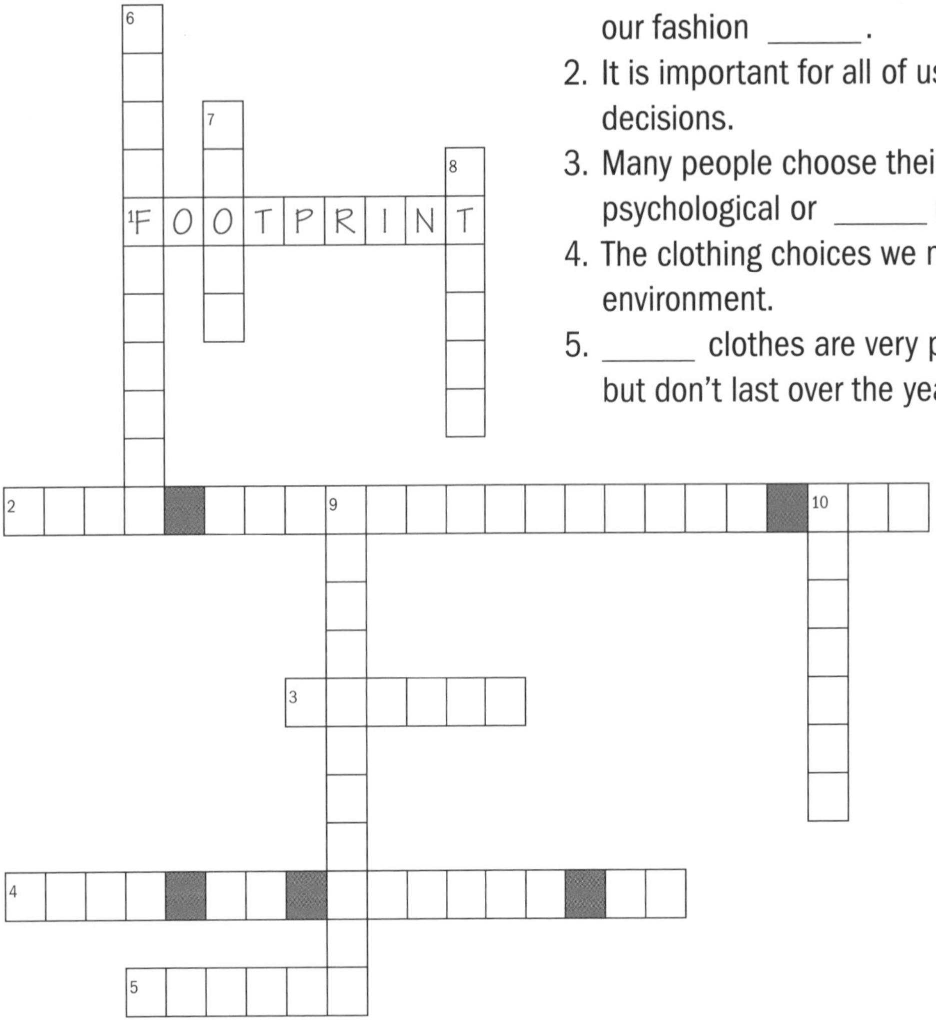

Across

1. Each of us should shop wisely in order to reduce our fashion ______.
2. It is important for all of us to ______ our clothing decisions.
3. Many people choose their clothes for psychological or ______ reasons.
4. The clothing choices we make ______ our environment.
5. ______ clothes are very popular for a short time, but don't last over the years.

Down

6. The ______ of nylon creates a powerful toxic greenhouse gas.
7. ______, such as cotton, use enormous amounts of water and pesticides.
8. ______ of clothing can be modern or traditional.
9. A person may wear different kinds of clothing to express his or her ______.
10. Many people like wearing the latest ______, because it's popular.

2 **Look at the photos.** Write one sentence about each. Use two words from the box in each sentence.

chemicals	cotton	crop	footprint	leather	material	synthetic

1. ______________________________

2. ______________________________

3 **Listen.** Think about what you have read in this unit. Circle **T** for *True* or **F** for *False*. 015

1. T F   2. T F   3. T F

4. T F   5. T F   6. T F

4 **Listen again.** Correct the false statements. 016

____

____

____

____

5 **Look at labels on four pieces of your own clothing.** Write down what they're made of. Then classify the materials as natural, synthetic or both. Use your dictionary as needed. Share your answers with a partner.

Item of clothing	Material(s)	Natural	Synthetic	Both
shoes	leather, rubber			✓

GRAMMAR

Present passive: Describing actions and processes

Active sentences	**Passive sentences**
Farmers grow cotton in warm climates.	Cotton is grown in warm climates.
Designers make many clothes from cotton.	Many clothes are made from cotton.
object	**subject**

The objects in the active sentences become the subjects of the passive sentences.

When we use the passive, we focus on the action performed, not on the person performing it. Most of the time, the person who performs the action is not important, or is not known. In some cases, when we want to mention who or what did the action, we use *by*.

The cotton **was picked by** *young volunteers. The cotton* **was picked by** *special machines.*

1 Change the active sentences to the present passive.

Cotton: From Plant to Thread

1. Workers pick the cotton from the fields.
   The cotton is picked from the fields.
2. Machines remove the seeds from the cotton.
3. People ship the cotton to textile mills.
4. Textile machines clean the cotton and separate it into smaller pieces.
5. People use special machines to separate the fibres.
6. These machines work the cotton into a kind of soft, untwisted rope.
7. More machines pull and twist the rope until it's thin.
8. Machines twist the fibres to make cotton thread.

2 **Write.** What happens to cotton after it becomes thread? Use the passive voice.

____

____

3 **Read and complete the sentences.** Use the appropriate verb form. Then listen and check. 017

apply	**check**	**cut off**	**own**	~~**place**~~	**spray**	**use**
attach	**cover**	**make**	**paint**	**ship**	**require**	**work**

In many shops, mannequins are used to show clothes. The best, most expensive mannequins are made in many different steps. Here are some of them.

1. A structure that supports clay ___is placed___ in the correct pose.
2. Wet clay ____________ into the correct shape on the structure.
3. The clay head, hands and feet ____________, or connected.
4. The arms and legs ____________ where the joints will be on the final mannequin.
5. All of the pieces ____________ with plaster to make a mould.
6. When the plaster mould is ready, it ____________ for any imperfections.
7. Next, the plaster mould ____________ to make a new resin mould.
8. A mannequin ____________ by adding a layer of gel to the new mould.
9. The gel ____________ with fibre-glass resin.
10. Next, the mannequin's skin ____________.
11. After the paint is dry, make-up ____________ to the face.
12. As a final step, the mannequin ____________ to the retailer.

A mannequin

1 **Listen and read.** As you read, notice similarities and differences between the two designers. 018

AMAZING ACCESSORIES

As a young girl, Madison Nicole Robinson spent a lot of time on the beaches where she grew up. At the age of eight, she drew a flip flop on paper and added sea characters that she created. When she showed her dad saying, 'Look Dad, FishFlops®!' he knew they would be a success.

Madison wrote to a big fashion retailer, who was very interested in selling her product. Madison's FishFlops® became immediately popular. The young entrepreneur soon appeared in online media and was interviewed on major news channels and in well-known business magazines.

Madison gives talks to inspire others to be creative, have a positive attitude and to never give up. She also believes in giving back. She has donated 20,000 pairs of FishFlops® to charities and children's hospitals. Part of the sales of her footwear at zoos and aquariums goes directly to protecting wildlife in danger.

Moziah Bridges ('Mo' for short) is another young entrepreneur with big ideas. When he was only nine years old, his grandmother gave him a sewing machine. It inspired him to design and sew colourful, eco-friendly bow ties from old fabrics.

Moziah's bow tie styles became trendy very quickly. With his mother's strong support, he started his own company called Mo's Bows. Since then, he has appeared in fashion and business magazines and on TV. Now a teenager, he has plans to design more than bow ties. He is currently developing a line of skinny ties and socks. In the future, he even hopes to design furniture for the home.

Mo's mother always told him to 'dream big now', and he is. He also helps others with their dreams. Moziah donates part of his profits from the sale of a special bow tie to fund a summer camp scholarship for children.

2 **Read and tick T for *True* or F for *False*.** Rewrite any false sentences as true.

	T	F
1. Mo's bow ties are eco-friendly because they're made of old fabrics.	☐	☐
2. Entrepreneurs aren't interested in business opportunities.	☐	☐
3. People who donate items expect to be paid for them.	☐	☐
4. Madison's company benefits children and animals.	☐	☐

____

____

____

3 **Read 'Amazing Accessories' again.** How are Madison and Mo similar? Different? Fill in the Venn diagram.

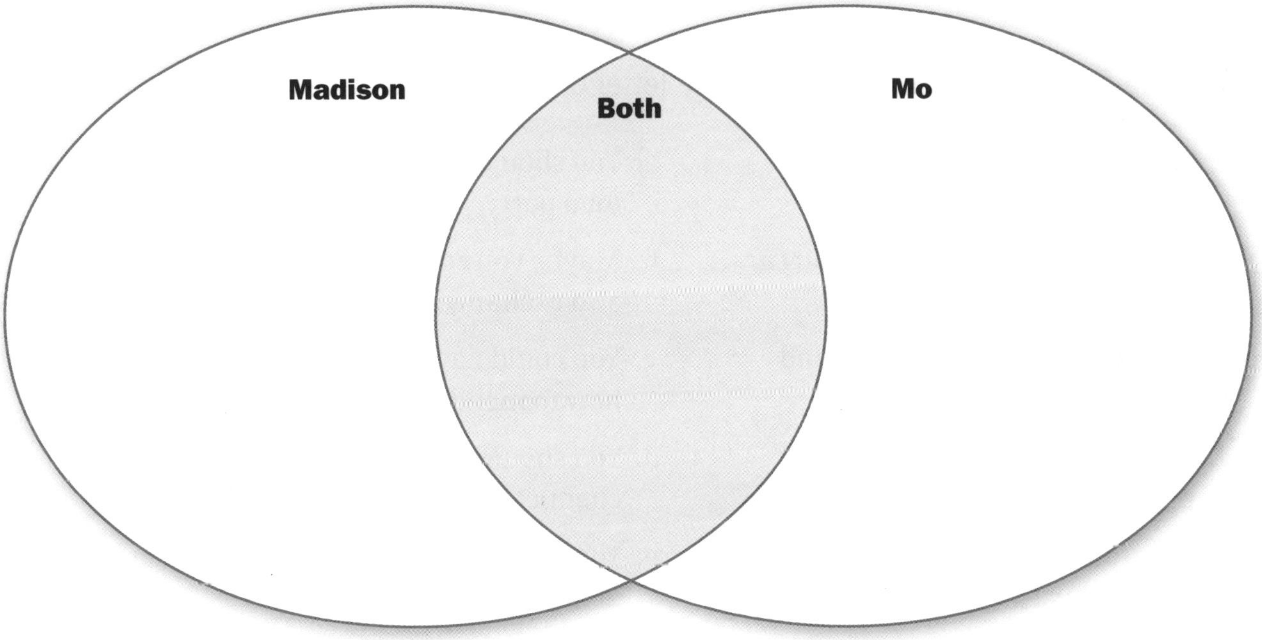

4 **You have now read about four young designers: Santana Draper, Maya Penn, Madison Robinson and Moziah Bridges.** Imagine you could work with one of them. Who would you choose to work with, and why?

____

____

____

____

____

GRAMMAR

Modals: Making suggestions and giving advice about present and past actions

PRESENT

could + verb	*should* + verb
We **could dry** these clothes in the sun. We **could save** on electricity.	You **should reduce** your fashion footprint. You **should recycle** your clothes.

PAST

Could have + past participle	*Should have* + past participle
You **could have saved** those jeans. You **could have made** them into shorts.	We **should have returned** that leather jacket. We **should have bought** the cotton jacket.

could + verb and *could have* + past participle are usually used to make suggestions
should + verb and *should have* + past participle are usually used to give advice

1 **Read and match the sentences.** Write the letter on the line.

_____ 1. Last year's clothes are too small for me now.

_____ 2. I'm going to dye this white shirt a nice bright red.

_____ 3. Look! I bought four T-shirts and got another one for free!

_____ 4. How does this outfit look for the party?

_____ 5. My green necklace broke, so I threw it away.

_____ 6. I don't like this shirt, but it was a birthday gift.

a. You shouldn't wear that. It's too casual for a party.

b. Maybe you could return it to the shop and exchange it.

c. You could have given it to me. I know how to mend jewellery.

d. You should use a natural dye, not toxic chemicals.

e. You could give them to a smaller friend or family member.

f. You shouldn't have bought them. You have too many already!

2 **Listen.** Write a comment for each situation. 019

1. ______________________________

2. ______________________________

3. ______________________________

4. ______________________________

5. ______________________________

6. ______________________________

3 **Read Lola's blog.** Write back to her and comment on her problems. Make suggestions and give advice.

Disaster day! I came home from football practice to find my room a total mess! My 7-year-old sister and 10-year-old brother looked through all my things, including my wardrobe. You won't believe what they did. My brother took the blanket from my bed and made a kind of tent-castle. Then he took my scarf collection and made a huge, long 'snake' with my scarves. My sister took all my clothes out of my wardrobe to make a princess outfit. Then my brother 'rescued' the princess from the snake that was attacking the castle. What a mess!

And that's not all. They brought their snacks with them. Now I have breadcrumbs everywhere and chocolate stains on my white skirt. And I still can't find one of my trainers. Now I want to go into their rooms and make a mess. Then they'll understand how it feels!

You should relax. They're only young. Be patient!

Your brother and sister seem creative! You should just have fun with them.

You could have told your brother and sister to stay out of your room.

____

____

____

____

____

WRITING

We use persuasive writing when we want to convince readers to adopt our opinion about an issue. Using facts and statistics helps make an argument stronger. Remember to use phrases such as these:

- according to ...
- ... points out that
- research shows that ...
- the facts show that ...
- recent studies support ...
- ... states that

1 Organise.

1. Your topic is *Reducing Our Fashion Footprint*. Look through Student's Book Unit 4 and find examples of facts and statistics that can support your position. Do some research on the Internet to find additional information. Make a list of your important facts and statistics here.

2. Plan your writing. You'll need an introductory paragraph with a topic sentence. Your topic sentence will state your main idea. Write your topic sentence here.

   ____

   You'll need two to three body paragraphs. Explain your position. Support it with facts and statistics.

   Finally, you'll need a concluding paragraph. It will summarise your main idea and include a 'call to action' on the part of your readers.

2 Write.

1. Go to page 71 in your book. Re-read the model and writing prompt.
2. Write your first draft. Check for organisation, content, punctuation, capitalisation and spelling.
3. Write your final draft. Share it with your teacher and classmates.

Now I can ...

· talk about fashion and my fashion footprint.

☐ Yes, I can!
☐ I think I can.
☐ I need more practice.

Why do you wear the clothes you wear?

____

What's one thing you could do to reduce your fashion footprint?

____

· use the present passive voice to describe processes.

☐ Yes, I can!
☐ I think I can.
☐ I need more practice.

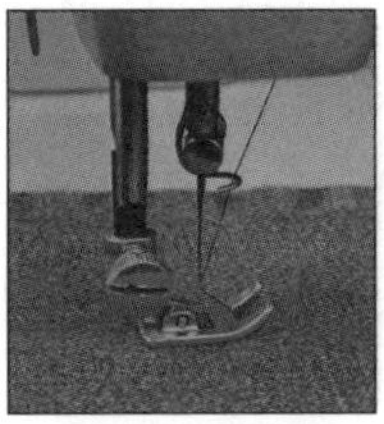

First, the jeans are assembled.

Then,

____
____
____
____

After that,

____
____
____
____

Finally, the jeans are purchased.

· use *could* and *could have* to make suggestions; use *should* and *should have* to give advice.

☐ Yes, I can!
☐ I think I can.
☐ I need more practice.

Read and respond to the comment below. Use a form of *could* or *should.*

I threw away all my old coats.

____

____

· present and support my opinion.

☐ Yes, I can!
☐ I think I can.
☐ I need more practice.

Wearing fur is (right / wrong) ______________ because

____

____

____

YOU DECIDE Choose an activity. Go to page 93.

Units 3–4 Review

1 **Read.** Choose the correct word to complete the sentences.

Working Together Like Geese

Every year, (1) _____ of geese (2) _____ to look for food and nesting locations. They fly in a V-shaped (3) _____.

Scientists have studied the (4) _____ behaviour of geese and realised what an (5) _____ it is. Geese can reach their destination more quickly and use less energy if they (6) _____ and fly together in this formation.

When geese fly together, each goose provides an extra upward lift for the goose flying behind it. This means that flying together in a V-formation (7) _____ the whole flock to fly 70 per cent further with the same amount of energy than if each goose flew alone.

When the goose in front of the formation (who uses the most energy) gets tired, it moves to the back of the group. Another goose then becomes the (8) _____ at the front.

If a goose becomes sick or injured during (9) _____, two geese will (10) _____ behind to look after the weak goose until it can fly.

It seems that geese can teach us a lot about teamwork and also about caring for each other's well-being.

1. a. herds b. flocks c. swarms
2. a. migrate b. breed c. hunt
3. a. circle b. formation c. crowd
4. a. crowd b. potential c. collective
5. a. energy b. area c. efficient system
6. a. assemble b. mimic c. prefer
7. a. assembles b. allows c. assumes
8. a. flock b. leader c. crowd
9. a. migration b. formation c. collection
10. a. wait for b. stand out c. remain

2 **Read the article.** Fill in each blank with the correct word. The first letter of each word is given.

Fleece jackets have become very (1) t_______________. They have traditionally been (2) w_______________ more by climbers, but now they are (3) p_______________ in cities too as they are warm and (4) a_______________.

Sadly, though, this outdoor jacket is not eco-(5) f_______________ and leaves a very negative (6) f_______________ on the environment.

The fleece jacket is full of tiny pieces of plastic that flow into our waterways and then into our rivers and oceans every time we wash it. These tiny pieces absorb dangerous (7) t_______________ chemicals like a sponge.

Fish think the microplastics are food and eat them. This eventually has an (8) i_______________ on our own food when the fish ends up on our dinner tables.

However, it's not just (9) s_______________ material that contains these plastics. They are also present in (10) m_______________ food products, soaps and toothpastes. Manufacturers need to take greater (11) r_______________, and we should also do our (12) p_______________ by choosing our food carefully.

3 **Listen.** Choose the best ending for each sentence. 020

1. When people heard the popular music, they ____ .
   a. assembled and started singing
   b. assembled and started dancing
2. It looked like the dancers were ____ .
   a. mimicking each other
   b. choosing a leader
3. There didn't seem to be ____ .
   a. a leader
   b. a co-ordinated formation
4. At first, there weren't ____ .
   a. enough people
   b. many people
5. More and more people ____ .
   a. stood up
   b. joined in
6. There was ____ .
   a. too much space
   b. not enough space
7. Carla ____ .
   a. got on the bus
   b. got off the bus
8. The friends ____ .
   a. joined the flash mob
   b. went off to talk

4 **Write.** Change each sentence so that the meaning is the same. Use the present passive for 1-4 and *could*, *should*, *could have* or *should have* for 5-8.

1. People use smartphones to scan barcodes.
   Smartphones ______________________________ .
2. Textile mills make half of all cotton collected into clothes.
   Half of all cotton collected ______________________________ .
3. Machines pull long pieces of dry cloth through a container of hot dye.
   Long pieces of dry cloth ______________________________ .
4. They advise farmers to use fewer toxic chemicals.
   Farmers ______________________________ .
5. One possibility is to buy your clothes without synthetic dyes.
   ______________________________ your clothes without synthetic dyes.
6. Why didn't you buy clothes without polyester and nylon?
   ______________________________ clothes without polyester and nylon.
7. It would be nice if she asked to borrow my hat.
   She ______________________________ to borrow my hat.
8. Why did you wash your woollen jumper in the machine? You ruined it!
   You ______________________________ your woollen jumper in the machine.

Unit 5

Flying High

1 **Read the clues.** Unscramble the words. Then decode the sentence and decide if it's true or false.

1. ighwet	__ __ [1] __ __ __	Measured in pounds or kilos
2. degli	__ [8] __ __ __	Float in the air
3. sapwnnig	__ __ [7] __ __ __ __ __	Distance between wing tips
4. tghifl	[12] __ __ __ __ __	The action of flying
5. wololh	[4] __ __ __ __ __	Empty
6. leray	__ __ __ __ [9]	Not late
7. oras	[3] __ __ __	Fly upward
8. tfuresea	__ [5] __ __ __ __ __ __	Characteristics
9. falp	__ __ [11] __	The movement of wings up and down
10. itmiled	__ __ [10] __ __ __ __	Not great or high in size or number
11. tatpadanio	__ __ __ __ [2] __ __ __ __ __	A change to improve life in an environment
12. ytilibapac	__ __ __ __ [13] __ __ __ __ __	The ability to do something
13. vevole	__ __ [6] __ __ __	Develop and improve over time

Write the letters according to the numbers to answer this question: *What is the only mammal to fly?*

[11]　[13] [11] [2]　[1] [3]　[2] [4] [5]　[6] [7] [8] [9]　[10] [11] [10] [10] [11] [8]

[2] [6]　[12] [8] [9].

Is this statement *true* or *false*? ____________________

2 **Complete the sentences with words from the box.** Then decide if the sentences are true or false based on the information on page 79 of your book.

adaptation	capability	evolved	features	hollow	limited	soar	weight	wingspan

	T	F
1. Animals haven't always had the ________________ to fly.	☐	☐
2. Wings probably ________________ from body features of insects' aquatic ancestors.	☐	☐
3. Mammals had an earlier ________________ to flight than reptiles.	☐	☐
4. Bats developed ________________ to help them fly.	☐	☐
5. Mammals learnt to fly because of their light, ________________ wings.	☐	☐
6. The ________________ of the first reptiles was over 10 metres (32 feet).	☐	☐
7. The wind helped reptiles ________________ and stay up in the air.	☐	☐
8. Adaptations over millions of years meant that mammals became lighter in ________________ .	☐	☐

3 **Listen.** Write the animal group and name of the animal being described. Complete the information. 021

1. **Animal group:** insect **Name:** ________________
   a. It can ________________ 150 times per second.
   b. The ________________ of its flight mechanism are among the most complex in the world.
   c. It is ________________ at controlling its flight.
2. **Animal group:** ________________ **Name:** ________________
   a. It has the ________________ of flying across half a football field.
   b. Its flight isn't ________________ by flapping wings but by skin on its side.
   c. The loose skin forms a cape and ________________ a safe landing.
3. **Animal group:** ________________ **Name:** ________________
   a. It's a myth that chickens aren't capable of ________________ .
   b. They can fly for a ________________ distance to escape predators.
   c. Farmers fatten up this bird. Its wings can't support its body ________________ .

GRAMMAR

Past perfect: Distinguishing the first of two actions in the past

Marco Polo described man-carrying kites.	Marco Polo **had already described** man-carrying kites by the time Fausto Veranizio designed a parachute.
Fausto Veranizio designed a parachute in 1595. Da Vinci drew a sketch of a parachute in 1485.	Long before Veranizio designed his parachute in 1595, Da Vinci **had drawn** a sketch of one.

We use the past perfect tense (***had/hadn't*** + past participle) to talk about a completed action that happened before another action in the past.

We can use certain time expressions with the past perfect, such as *long before, before, by the time* and *until that time.*

1 **Complete the sentences.** Pay attention to which activity happened first.

1. By the time the Chinese ________________ (experiment) with kites 2,500 years ago, animal flight ________________ (exist) for millions of years.
2. Long before the Chinese ________________ (start) flying kites, early humans ________________ (try) to imitate birds.
3. The Chinese ________________ (use) kites for measuring and signalling before people ________________ (try) to use them for transportation.
4. Although originally the Chinese ________________ (design) kites for military uses, they later ________________ (use) them for fun and entertainment.
5. Before paper ________________ (make) kites cheaper, the Chinese royal family ________________ (fly) silk kites.

2 **Listen to the ancient Greek myth.** Number the events in order. 022

____ a. He and his son were imprisoned in a tower.

____ b. His son flew too close to the sun.

____ c. Daedalus was exiled to Crete.

____ d. He had a son and named him Icarus.

__1__ e. Daedalus committed a crime.

____ f. The sea is named after Daedalus's son.

____ g. Daedalus designed wings.

____ h. Daedalus designed a labyrinth.

____ i. Icarus fell into the sea.

____ j. They escaped.

3 **Listen again.** Complete the sentences. Use the past perfect forms of the verbs from the box. 023

allow	**ascend**	**commit**	**design**	**forget**	**jump**	**observe**

1. Daedalus was exiled to Crete because he ________________ a crime.
2. He ________________ a labyrinth so King Minos could imprison the Minotaur.
3. Although Daedalus and his son had been imprisoned in a tower, wings ________________ them to escape.
4. Before they took flight, they ________________ out of the tower.
5. Icarus fell into the sea because he ________________ his father's words and he ________________ too close to the sun.

4 **Complete the story.** Circle the correct word and write the verbs in the past perfect tense.

Daedalus was a (1) **skilled** / **stable** architect who (2) ________________ (design) many great works. He was imprisoned with his son in a tower for showing his (3) **drawings** / **weight** and (4) **forces** / **features** of a labyrinth. From the tower, Daedalus observed how birds were adapted to (5) **weight** / **flight** with the help of wings. Daedalus and his son (6) ________________ (fly) like birds and escaped. Daedalus warned his son not to (7) **descend** / **ascend** too close to the sea or to (8) **ascend** / **descend** too close to the sun. However, Icarus powered himself towards the sun by (9) **supporting** / **flapping** his wings. The wings weren't (10) **stable** / **skilled** because the wax melted and the (11) **force** / **weight** of gravity gradually pulled him down. Poor Icarus! Things might have been different if his father (12) ________________ (design) a (13) **wingspan** / **parachute** instead!

1 **Listen and read.** As you read, notice how aerial vehicles have evolved. 024

Reach *for the* Remote Control

Even before 1903, when the Wright Brothers' dream of human flight had finally come true, remotely controlled aircraft were being tested mainly by the military. For example, during the American Civil War (1861–1865), the military used unmanned (no pilot) hot-air balloons to carry bombs. This wasn't successful partly because of weather conditions. Later, in 1883, the first photo from the air was taken using a kite, a camera and a very long piece of string.

People have been piloting planes for over 100 years, so it makes sense that flight is now evolving into machines that don't need pilots, such as Unmanned Aerial Vehicles (UAVs), or drones. These machines with no pilots are becoming more and more popular.

UAVs mainly come in three sizes. There are large vehicles that might one day carry passengers without pilots and medium-sized ones that are very similar to those used by the military. Then there are much smaller ones, such as quadcopters, that can fit in the palm of your hand.

Many people are nervous about the idea of a plane without a human. But there are already driverless trains between airport terminals and robo-trains in the subways of many cities. We're slowly adapting to automation.

Medium-sized UAVs, or drones, are very useful. They act like cameras in the sky. They're used for observing wildlife, monitoring protected areas and mapping ecosystems and farmland.

Advances in technology mean that smaller drones have greater capabilities. Quadcopters have four rotors that allow them to ascend, descend and do many different movements. People are only now beginning to realise their full potential. They can be sent into disaster areas or damaged buildings to look for people who are injured or trapped. They can search for chemical leaks, or check pollution levels and they can also be used in new construction.

UAVs have been described as flying smartphones. Maybe one day we'll see them everywhere, like pigeons in a city!

2 **Write.** Answer the questions.

1. How is this article different from the article on page 89 of your book?

2. What is a remotely controlled aircraft?

3. What was the first remotely controlled aircraft used for?

4. Are UAVs now used more in the military or in everyday life?

5. Why are some people nervous about the future of airlines?

6. How can UAVs help the environment?

7. How do you think a quadcopter might be useful in a damaged building?

3 **On the timeline, show the evolution of the UAV before and after the Wright Brothers' first flight.**

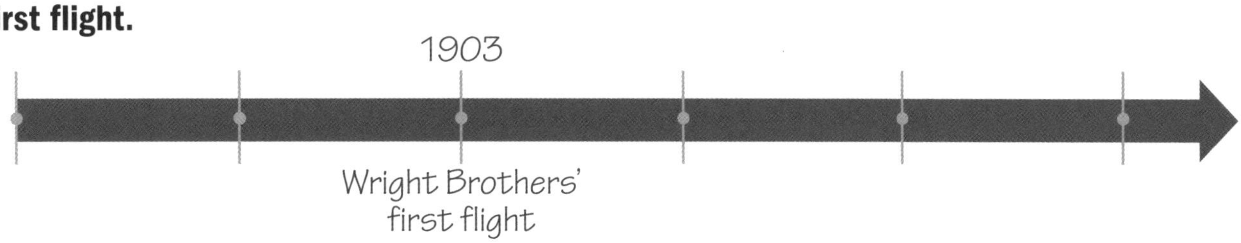

4 **Write.** Imagine that you had your own drone. How would you use it?

GRAMMAR

Past perfect continuous: Describing the first of two actions in the past

Animals **had been gliding** long before they learnt to fly.
Before they designed a powered plane, the Wright Brothers **had been designing** gliders.
He **had been controlling** the plane with a remote control before it crashed.

We use the past perfect continuous (***had/hadn't*** + ***been*** + past participle) to describe a continuous action (something that had been happening), before another action in the past.

1 **Listen.** Complete the sentences using the past perfect continuous. 025

1. Before Ryan was seven, he ______________________ pictures of how birds fly.
2. Before modern-day flight existed, Leonardo da Vinci ______________________ on the same topic.
3. Before Ryan became inspired by the capabilities of new technologies, he ______________________ how dinosaurs may have moved.
4. Eight years before his research into the colour of the *Archaeopteryx* feather, Ryan ______________________ in a band called Icarus.
5. While Ryan ______________________ a tattoo, the tattoo artist identified the *Archaeopteryx* feather.

2 **Answer the questions about yourself.** Use the past perfect continuous.

1. Before this school year, how long had you been going to your school?
   ____
2. Before you started this year, how many years had you been studying English?
   ____
3. Before you started this activity, how long had you been sitting at your desk?
   ____
4. Before you started this activity, what had you been doing?
   ____

3 **Read the letter of complaint.** Underline words connected to flight. Then answer the questions.

Is my neighbour allowed to fly his UAV over my garden?

Yesterday, I was watching a documentary for a school assignment when I noticed something flying by the window. I thought it was my neighbour's football.

And then, when I went to the kitchen to get some water, I heard an engine and saw something soaring over the fence. It was a remote-controlled quadcopter! It descended quickly and I saw the 'pilot' as it landed in my neighbour's garden. I went out and he explained that he is allergic to cats and, for months, had been trying to scare a cat away. He'd tried putting hot pepper on the grass and plastic forks in the flowerbeds, but nothing worked!

The day before, he'd been using the quadcopter at work to take aerial photos of traffic. That's when he got the idea of using it to scare the cat away.

As I returned to my assignment, I heard the quadcopter take off again. I saw the cat come out of a flowerbed and jump over the fence into my garden. The UAV followed from above. Can my neighbour keep doing this?

Jonas

1. What had Jonas been doing when he saw something outside the window?

____

____

2. What had he been doing when he heard the sound of an engine?

____

____

3. What had his neighbour been doing for months?

____

____

4. How had his neighbour been using the quadcopter before flying it above Jonas's garden?

____

____

WRITING

When we write a classification essay, we first introduce the topic (e.g., restaurant) in an introductory paragraph. Then, we divide the topic into categories (fast-food, vegetarian, seafood and so on). Each category gets its own paragraph. In each paragraph, we describe the shared characteristics that make up the category. Finally, we include a conclusion in which we bring the categories back together again to talk about the main topic.

1 Organise.

1. Your task is to describe two types of animal flight. Look back at the descriptions of flight in different animals in Unit 5 of your book. If you prefer, do some research on the Internet to find other examples. Choose two animals and make notes about their flight characteristics in the table.

Animal 1	Animal 2

2. Plan your writing. You'll need an introductory paragraph. Here you will state which two animals you are going to describe. Include your topic sentence in the introductory paragraph. Write your topic sentence here:

   ____

   You'll need one body paragraph describing the flight of one animal and a second body paragraph describing the flight of the second animal. Support your description with facts.

   Finally, you'll need a concluding paragraph. You'll need to make a statement about the two animals you've chosen and about the topic in general.

2 Write.

1. Go to page 89 in your book. Re-read the model.
2. Write your first draft. Check for organisation, content, punctuation, capitalisation and spelling.
3. Check your final draft. Share it with your teacher and classmates.

Now I can ...

- **talk about the evolution of flying animals and machines.**

☐ Yes, I can!
☐ I think I can.
☐ I need more practice.

How did flight evolve in animals?

How did flying machines evolve?

- **use the past perfect to distinguish the first of two actions in the past.**

☐ Yes, I can!
☐ I think I can.
☐ I need more practice.

Rewrite the sentences to show which action came first.

Dinosaurs became extinct. Birds became skilled fliers.

Fausto Veranizio designed a man-carrying parachute in 1595. George Cayley designed the first stable glider to carry a human.

- **use the past perfect continuous to describe the first of two actions in the past.**

☐ Yes, I can!
☐ I think I can.
☐ I need more practice.

Write two sentences using the past perfect continuous. Use the words in the box.

drive	drone	rain	slippery

- **write a classification essay to describe two types of animal flight.**

☐ Yes, I can!
☐ I think I can.
☐ I need more practice.

How is flight in bats different from flight in birds?

YOU DECIDE Choose an activity. Go to page 94.

Unit 6

New Frontiers

1 **Complete the sentences.** Then fill in the crossword.

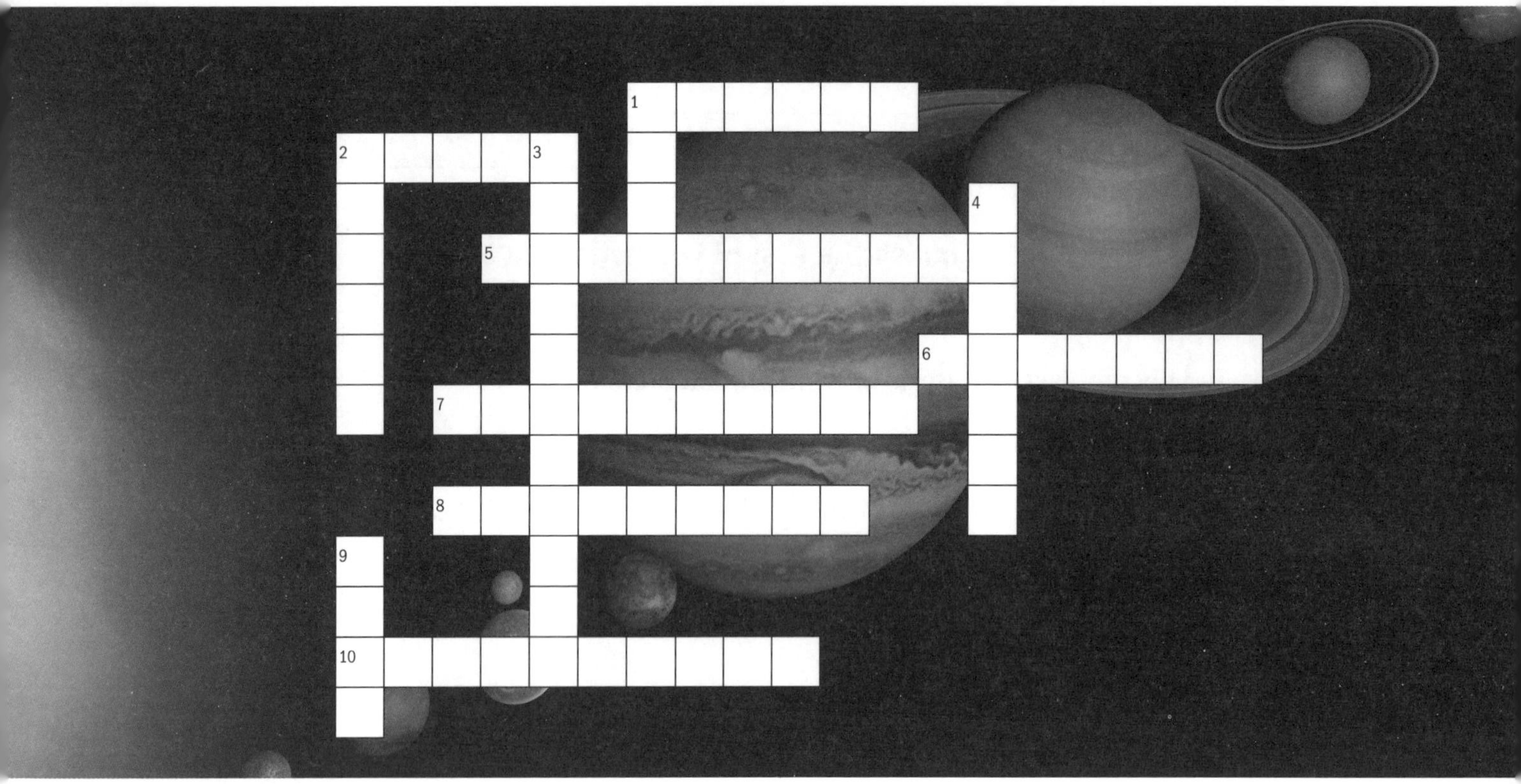

Down

1. The desert seems to have no end. It's so __________________ .
2. Many cereal crops are grown on __________________ because they are flat.
3. Water and oxygen are __________________ to life.
4. Life and water are __________________ that fascinate scientists.
9. After the __________________ storm, they had to clean their roofs and windows.

Across

1. The river ran along the __________________ between the mountains.
2. There is now __________________ that water really does exist on Mars.
5. __________________ are tools or devices that help scientists do their work.
6. Temperatures reach 70 __________________ Fahrenheit in the summer on Mars.
7. Earth is surrounded by an __________________ made up of different gases.
8. The moon's __________________ is full of craters.
10. __________________ orbit the Earth and send back information.

2 **What aspects of Earth and Mars are similar?** What aspects are different? Re-read pages 94 and 95 in your book and use your own knowledge to fill in the Venn diagram.

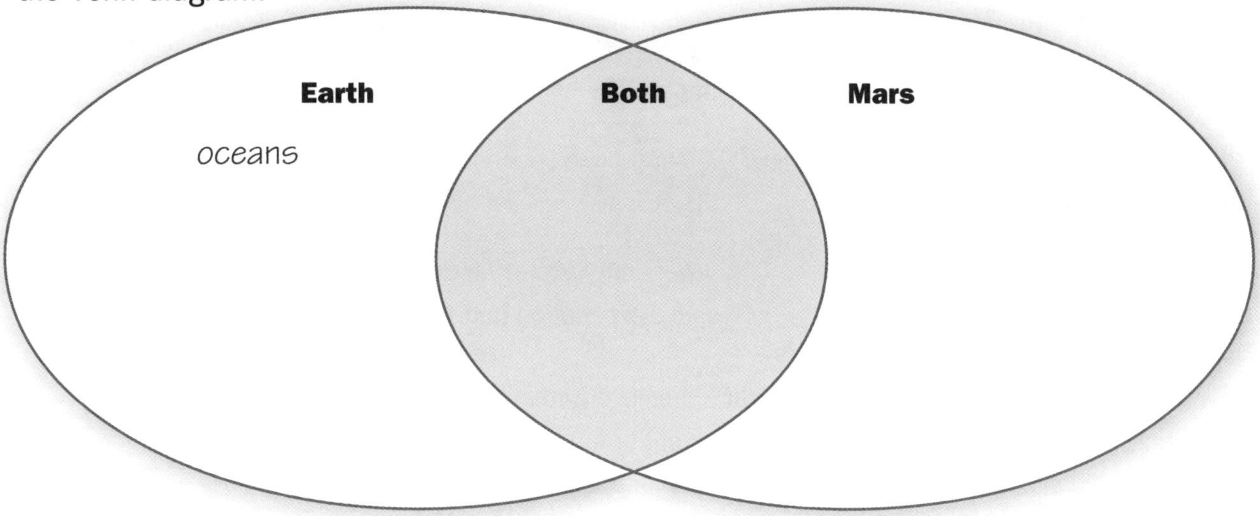

3 **Listen to the information.** Answer the questions. 026

1. Who was Clyde Tombaugh?

____

2. What did the New Horizons spacecraft detect?

____

3. What was the Mars rover, Curiosity, equipped with?

____

4. What were Sputnik and Explorer 1?

____

5. How much oxygen is there in Mars's atmosphere?

____

6. What might stop tourists from visiting Mars in future?

____

7. What is the temperature at the equator on Mars at midday in summer?

____

GRAMMAR

Present and past conditionals: Talking about unlikely (but possible) or impossible situations

Unlikely but possible	Impossible
If there **were** life on Mars, we **would know** about it by now.	If it **had been** less hazy, we **would have seen** the eclipse.
If we **visited** Mars, we **would find** some aspects similar to those on Earth.	Rovers **might have landed** on Mars sooner if space exploration **had received** more money.

We use ***if*** + past simple, ***would/could/might*** + infinitive (without *to*) to talk about events and situations that are unlikely to happen in the present or future. After *I*, *he*, *she* or *it*, use *were*: *If I* ***were*** *an astronaut, I would travel to the International Space Station.*

We use ***if*** + past perfect, ***would/could/might have*** + past participle to talk about impossible or hypothetical events and situations in the past.

The *if*-clause can come first or second in the sentence. When it comes second, no comma is needed: *I would travel to Mars* ***if*** *it were possible.*

1 **Match the sentence halves.** Write the letter on the line.

_____ 1. If there were tours into space,
_____ 2. If I had had a good telescope,
_____ 3. If I had been more curious at school,
_____ 4. If I lived in the United States,
_____ 5. If I were a millionaire,
_____ 6. If scientists had discovered life on Mars,

a. I would build my own spacecraft and satellite.
b. I might have seen Pluto.
c. I would visit Pluto.
d. I would have asked for proof.
e. I could have become an astronomer.
f. I would definitely visit one of NASA's visitor centres.

2 **Listen to the film summary.** Complete the sentences with a conditional. Then choose words from the box to complete the remaining blanks. Circle the two sentences that are false and explain how you know. 027

astronomy	geysers	habitable	hazy	satellite	seasonal dust

1. If the team ________________ (know) about the ________________ storms, they probably ________________ (stay) inside the base camp.
2. If the weather ________________ (be) less ________________, the team ________________ (continue) their search.
3. The mission control centre ________________ (rescue) the scientist if they ________________ (have) a ________________ ready to put into space.
4. If the scientist ________________ (study) botany, he ________________ (plant) vegetables.
5. If Mars ________________ (be) habitable, the potatoes ________________ (grow) outside.
6. He ________________ (have) a shower, if Mars ________________ (have) ________________ or rivers.
7. The reviewer says that if teenagers ________________ (see) the film, they ________________ (want) to study chemistry, geology and ________________.

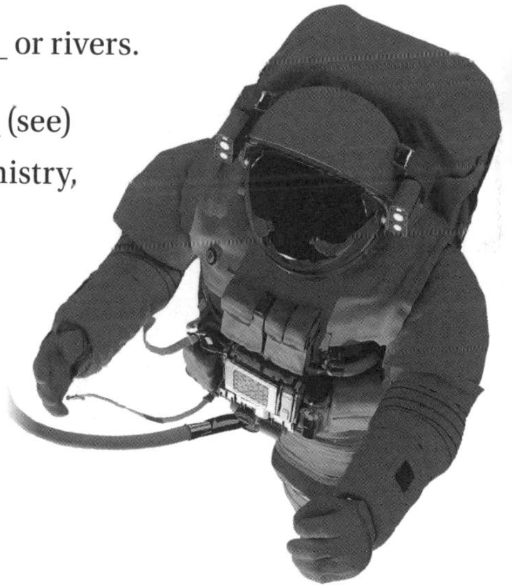

3 **Write an appropriate ending for each sentence.**

1. If more planets had been habitable, ________________.
2. If the temperature were 30 degrees C (87°F), ________________.
3. If the diameter of Earth were greater, ________________.
4. If I lived on a plain, ________________.
5. If a dust storm had suddenly hit my town, ________________.
6. If my car had been equipped with the technology to travel into the past, ________________.

1 **Listen and read.** As you read, notice the sequence of different things that need to happen to make the rover move. 028

Driving on Mars

A high-tech rover with a vast, red, rocky landscape in the background is now a familiar image. Curiosity is the latest rover on Mars. It cost over US$2 billion to build and it is equipped with highly advanced instruments. This technology and the actual voyage to Mars are already incredible. But have you ever wondered how you actually drive a rover on a planet several million miles away?

Well, a sequence of things needs to happen during the Martian night, while the rover is 'asleep'. A team of about 200 scientists on Earth analyses information that the rover sends back. They discuss what needs to be done next and which instruments will be used. The work is complicated because the scientists need to calculate how much power each instrument will use. Because there are so many instruments, this takes time.

The team writes thousands of lines of computer code to instruct the rover. They map out the best, smoothest route to the next destination. They include where the rover will stop to take pictures or operate an instrument.

Fortunately, the scientists' laboratory has an outside area called the Mars Yard. It's full of sand, dust and rocks of different sizes. Engineers use this area to test software and movements on two Curiosity models and solve any problems they may have.

Every day, a signal is sent to 'wake up' the rover and upload its instructions. This is also complex. The Mars day is 40 minutes longer than an Earth day, which means the working day and the time when the information is sent are continually changing.

Distance is another challenge. Signals between Earth and Mars have to cross up to 250 million miles (401 million kilometres) of space. What is more, the signal isn't direct. It has to go through communication satellites, which takes time.

There's a lot of pressure to get things right on Mars, but the one easy thing about driving on an empty planet is that you don't have any traffic coming from the other direction!

2 **Read.** Choose each correct answer.

1. The text is about ____ .
   a. how the rover's instruments work
   b. how the rover knows what to do

2. While the rover 'sleeps', ____ .
   a. scientists prepare the next day's instructions
   b. scientists also sleep

3. The team of scientists ____ .
   a. programme every movement and task
   b. let the rover make its own decisions

4. Scientists have ____ .
   a. a virtual landscape to practise the rover's movements
   b. a physical space to practise the rover's movements

5. An Earth day is ____ .
   a. longer than a day on Mars
   b. shorter than a day on Mars

6. Signals to the rover ____ .
   a. go through satellites
   b. are direct

3 **Use the organiser below to complete the sequence of how instructions are given to the rover.**

scientists analyse data and have meetings → ____ → ____ → ____ → the rover wakes up and follows instructions

4 **Write.** If you were one of the scientists, what would be the greatest challenge for you? Give your reasons.

____

____

____

____

GRAMMAR

Adverbs: Comparing how things are done

The instruments detected water **accurately**.	Curiosity has travelled **far** on the plains of the red planet.
The instruments worked **as accurately as** scientists had hoped.	Curiosity goes **as far as** scientists want it to.
The instruments detected water **more accurately than** before.	The rover Endeavor has travelled **further than** Curiosity.
The instruments on Curiosity detected water **the most accurately**.	Endeavor has travelled **the furthest** of all rovers so far.

With comparative adverbs, use ***more ... than***; with superlative adverbs, use ***the most***. With adverbs that have the same form as the adjectives, use ***-er*** and ***-est***: ***fast***, ***faster***, ***fastest***; ***hard***, ***harder***, ***hardest***; ***near***, ***nearer***, ***nearest***.

There are some irregular forms: ***well***, ***better***, ***best***; ***badly***, ***worse***, ***worst***; ***far***, ***further***, ***furthest***.

1 **Listen to each pair of sentences.** Then make changes to the adjective to complete each sentence with the correct use of the adverb. 029

1. Astronauts eat ________________ than I do. (healthy)
2. I think astronauts sleep ________________ at home. (good)
3. Do dust storms happen on Mars ________________ hurricanes on Earth? (seasonal)
4. Voyager 1 and 2 have travelled ________________ in the solar system. (far)
5. The rovers Spirit and Curiosity found water ________________ scientists expected. (quick)
6. Scientists prepare the rover's movements ________________ they can. (careful)

2 **Write.** Use adverbs to describe how you do things compared to your friends or other members of your family.

When I go cycling with friends, I can go the fastest.

____

3 **Read.** Underline all the uses of adverbs comparing how things are done. Then answer the questions.

If I could go anywhere in space, I would go to Pluto. We haven't known much about Pluto until now. Even the Hubble Space Telescope couldn't take pictures of Pluto as clearly as the latest space probe, New Horizons.

New Horizons was launched in 2006. It took nine and a half years to reach Pluto. New Horizons travels faster than any other spacecraft. It can travel a million miles a day! Although the probes Voyager 1 and 2 have travelled the furthest in space, they didn't travel to Pluto as closely as New Horizons.

A team of scientists on Earth produced the most accurately planned sequence of instructions available so that the probe could make hundreds of observations as it flew by Pluto. It sent back the most incredibly amazing photos. Although New Horizons is now further away than Pluto, the small planet is starting to share its secrets.

1. What took the best pictures of Pluto, the Hubble Space Telescope or New Horizons?

____

2. How does the speed of New Horizons compare with other spacecraft?

____

3. What didn't Voyager 1 and 2 do as well as New Horizons?

____

4. How did a team of scientists on Earth make sure the probe could make good observations as it flew by Pluto?

____

5. Where is New Horizons now?

____

WRITING

We use persuasive writing when we want to persuade, or convince, our readers to agree with our opinion. One way to organise this type of essay is by presenting both sides of the argument, point by point. Present one argument and then present your counter-argument in the same paragraph.

In the next paragraph, do the same. Present another argument and then present your counter-argument. Remember to use conjunctions such as *but*, *however*, *although* and *in contrast* to link your ideas.

1 Organise.

1. Your task is to write about the argument that it's better to explore the ocean than outer space. To persuade your readers, research facts to support your argument.

	Ocean Exploration	Space Exploration
Argument		
Counter-argument		

2. In your first paragraph, introduce the two arguments you're going to discuss. Write a topic sentence to lead your reader into your essay. Write your topic sentence here.

   ____

   You'll need at least two paragraphs. In each, present the argument and then your counter-argument.

   The last line of your essay should make it clear which argument you support.

2 Write.

1. Go to page 105 in your book. Re-read the model and writing prompt.
2. Write your first draft. Check for organisation, content, punctuation, capitalisation and spelling.
3. Write your final draft. Share it with your teacher and classmates.

Now I can ...

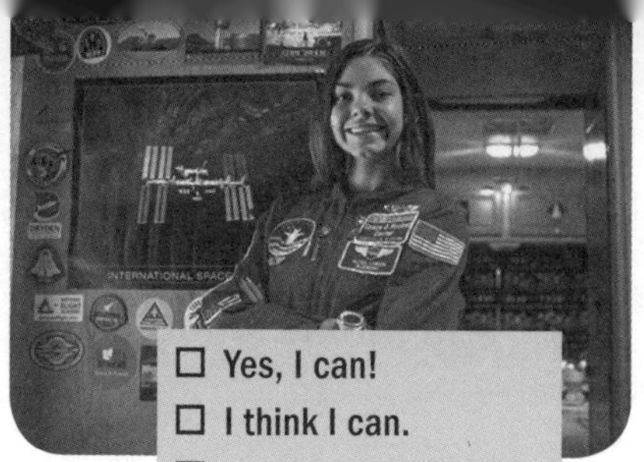

- **talk about space exploration.**

☐ Yes, I can!
☐ I think I can.
☐ I need more practice.

What do you think makes space exploration so exciting?

____

____

Would you like to be a space explorer? Why or why not?

____

____

- **use present and past conditionals to talk about unlikely (but possible) or impossible situations.**

☐ Yes, I can!
☐ I think I can.
☐ I need more practice.

1. Write a conditional sentence about something that is unlikely to happen in the present.

____

2. Write a conditional sentence that expresses an unlikely situation in the past.

____

- **use adverbs to compare how things are done.**

☐ Yes, I can!
☐ I think I can.
☐ I need more practice.

1. Scientists can drive a rover in space ____________ (easily) a car on Earth.
2. New Horizons has taken ____________ (amazingly) detailed photos of Pluto.
3. We know our solar system ____________ (better) ever before.

- **write a persuasive essay about space and ocean exploration.**

☐ Yes, I can!
☐ I think I can.
☐ I need more practice.

Present a counter-argument for each statement.

Space exploration is important because we can learn a lot about the universe.

____

____

Ocean exploration can help us find new minerals.

____

____

YOU DECIDE Choose an activity. Go to page 95.

Units 5–6 Review

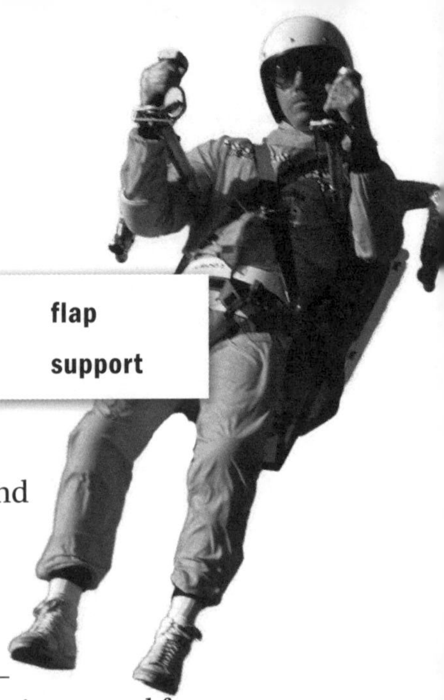

1 Read. Choose words from the box to complete the sentences.

allow	capability	descend	engines	evolve	flap
flight	limited	skilled	soaring	stable	support

The day when we can all have our own jet packs to ascend and (1) ________________ wherever we want may be closer than we think.

Up until now, jet packs only had the (2) ________________ of remaining in the air for a few seconds. Now that jet packs have improved features and smaller (3) ________________, companies are racing to bring a practical jet pack out onto the market. Of course, the first jet packs won't be cheap. They'll cost around $150,000, so their use will be (4) ________________ by price.

So it may still be some time before our airways are full of (5) ________________ jet packs. It's predicted that the first public use of jet packs will be at special (6) ________________ 'clubs' where people can rent them and be taught how to use them by (7) ________________ trainers.

Businesses will probably be the first to use jet packs commercially, possibly for flying to meetings or delivering products. Jet packs could also (8) ________________ people who work in emergency services, including paramedics and firefighters, to travel across cities and provide help and (9) ________________ quickly.

As the possibilities (10) ________________, it's good to know that whatever happens, there are no wings to (11) ________________. That would be exhausting!

2 Listen. Circle each best answer. 030

1. In 2015, we discovered that our solar system is *full of dust / not such a cold, dark place.*
2. Pluto has a landscape with *plains of solid nitrogen / salt lakes.*
3. For 85 years, we only had *a hazy picture of Pluto / an artist's impression of Pluto.*
4. One of Saturn's moons has *seasonal dust storms / geysers.*
5. Thanks to a lander's solar panels, we saw *the planet Neptune / aspects of a comet.*
6. Scientists now have proof that there was once *a vast ancient ocean / life* on Mars.

3 **Read the situations.** Write sentences using the past perfect or past perfect continuous with the words in brackets.

1. Voyager 1 and 2 did not get as close to Pluto as New Horizons. (travel/furthest/space)
   They had travelled the furthest in space.
2. Bats learnt to fly 55 million years ago. (insects/fly/for millions of years before that)
   ____
3. Pterosaur were flying reptiles. (learn/fly/before birds)
   ____
4. A small probe landed on a comet. (travel/through space/many years)
   ____
5. Scientists were excited. (discover/water/Mars)
   ____

4 **Read.** Use forms of the words in brackets to complete the sentences.

1. If I ______________ (live) 6,000 years ago, I ______________ (see) different species of animals.
2. We ______________ (not, see) photos of Pluto if the space mission ______________ (fail).
3. The New Horizons probe is going ______________ (far) any spacecraft before it.
4. Scientists have been waiting ______________ (patient) anyone for results.
5. The Rosetta probe had to go ______________ (fast) the comet to travel beside it.

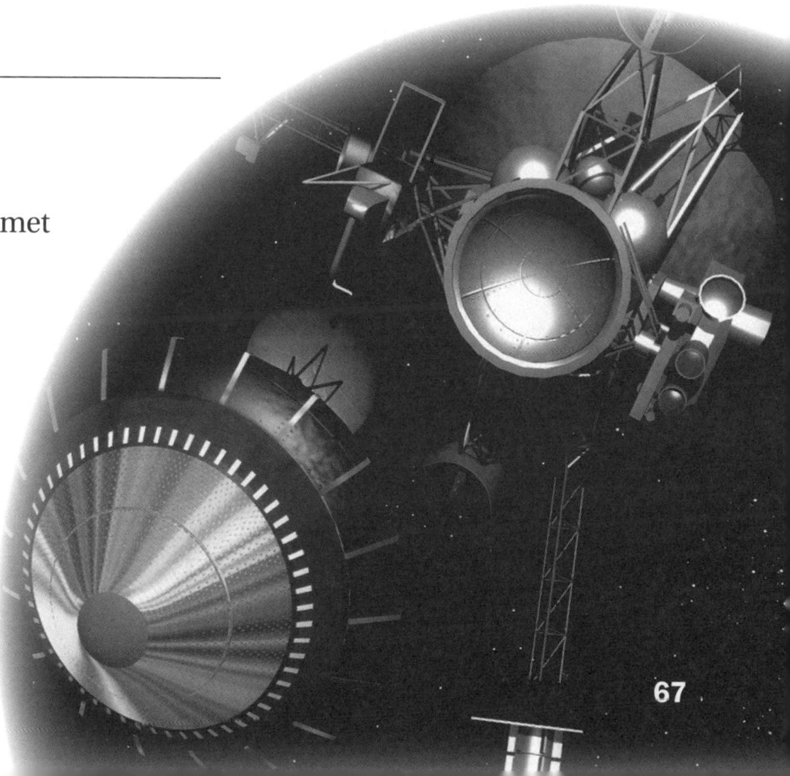

Unit 7

Visual Stories

1 **Complete each sentence with a word from the box.** Then match each picture to the correct sentence. Write the number.

audience	meaningful	oral	shock	subject	visual	witness

1.

2.

3.

4.

5.

6.

______ a. The student gave an ____________________ presentation with images on a screen.

______ b. The ____________________ saw the thief stealing the canvas.

______ c. The painting was ____________________ to her.

______ d. The ____________________ showed their anger when the artist didn't appear.

______ e. The image portrayed a man who was in ____________________ .

______ f. Her dogs were the ____________________ of her portraits.

2 **Read each definition and write the word.** Then use the letters in the circles to spell the name of a famous artist.

1. An image, usually of somebody's head and shoulders (___) ___ ___ ___ ___ ___ ___ ___
2. Something that is very important and significant ___ ___ ___ ___ (___) ___ ___ ___ ___ ___
3. Special cloth to paint on (___) ___ ___ ___ ___ ___
4. The people who watch, read or listen to something (___) ___ ___ ___ ___ ___ ___ ___
5. Someone who sees something happen ___ ___ ___ ___ ___ (___) (___)
6. Spoken, not written (___) ___ ___ ___

The famous artist is ___ ___ ___ ___ ___ ___ ___.

3 **Listen.** Complete the notes with a vocabulary word. Tick **T** for *True* or **F** for *False* for each sentence. Then, in your notebook, rewrite the false statements to make them true.

031

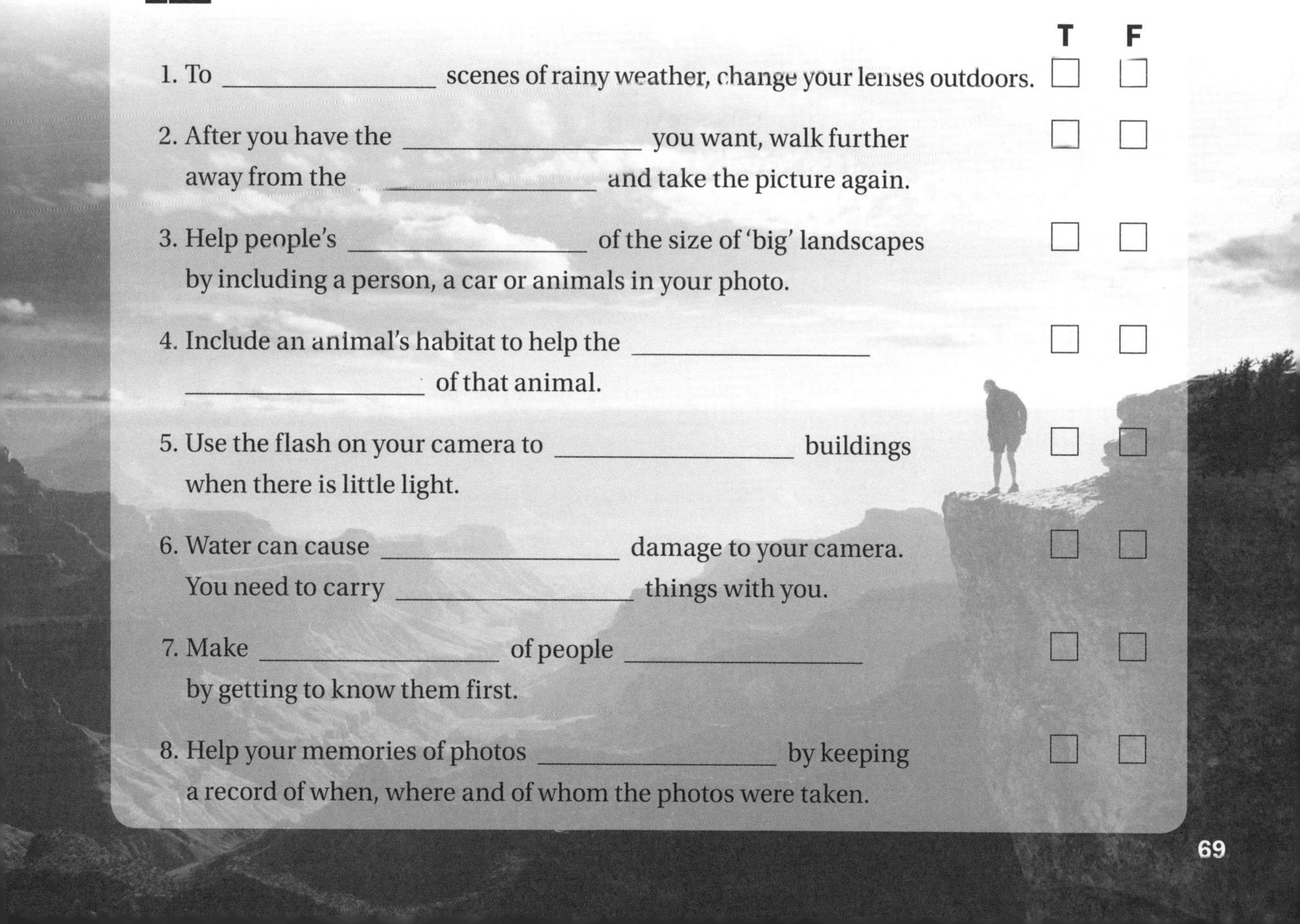

	T	F
1. To ________________ scenes of rainy weather, change your lenses outdoors.	☐	☐
2. After you have the ________________ you want, walk further away from the ________________ and take the picture again.	☐	☐
3. Help people's ________________ of the size of 'big' landscapes by including a person, a car or animals in your photo.	☐	☐
4. Include an animal's habitat to help the ________________ ________________ of that animal.	☐	☐
5. Use the flash on your camera to ________________ buildings when there is little light.	☐	☐
6. Water can cause ________________ damage to your camera. You need to carry ________________ things with you.	☐	☐
7. Make ________________ of people ________________ by getting to know them first.	☐	☐
8. Help your memories of photos ________________ by keeping a record of when, where and of whom the photos were taken.	☐	☐

GRAMMAR

Past passive: Describing past actions and processes

Thieves stole a Gauguin painting 40 years ago.	A Gauguin painting **was stolen** by thieves 40 years ago.
Picasso revolutionised art.	Art **was revolutionised** by Picasso.
Art dealers sold paintings for millions of dollars.	Paintings **were sold** by art dealers for millions of dollars.

When we use the passive, we usually focus on the action performed, not on the person performing it. However, when we use the past passive, it's more common to focus on the thing or person performing the action. We do this by using *by*. This is especially true when we talk about artwork and important discoveries.

The passive is more common in formal writing and less frequent in conversation.

To form the past passive, use ***was/were*** + past participle.

1 **Rewrite each sentence in the past passive so that the meaning is the same.**

1. Researchers found simply painted rocks from 10,000 years ago.

   Simply painted rocks from thousands of years ago ______________________.

2. Our ancestors recorded history in a permanent way through paintings.

   History ______________________.

3. Paintings told stories about the past before cameras.

   Before cameras, stories ______________________.

4. Ancient civilizations painted and decorated their ceramic pottery with stories.

   Ceramic pottery ______________________

   ______________________.

5. In the past, people made things to last.

   In the past, things ______________________.

2 **Listen.** Complete the sentences with words from the box and the past passive of the verbs in brackets. 032

abstract	canvas	landscape	masterpiece	permanent	quality	shock	witnesses

1. The ________________ *Guernica* ________________ (paint) by Pablo Picasso.
2. The town of Guernica ________________ (bomb) by the German air force.
3. The ________________ of war ________________ (portray) in the painting.
4. More than 1,600 people ________________ (kill).
5. The town and ________________ ________________ (destroyed).
6. Reports by ________________ ________________ (print) in the newspapers.
7. A mural-size ________________ ________________ (use) for the painting.
8. The subjects ________________ (show) in a new ________________ style.
9. The painting ________________ (return) to Spain in 1981 where it now has a ________________ home.

3 **Write.** Choose a painting by an artist you admire. Find out more about it. Use the past passive and the vocabulary in the box in Activity 2 to write about the painting.

My painting is ________________________ by ________________________.

____

____

____

____

____

____

1 **Listen and read.** Are you familiar with all the different ways stories can be portrayed? 033

THE WORLD IS A SCREEN

People have always illustrated stories on some sort of screen. First, we had cave walls. Now, we have tablets, smartphones, televisions and cinema screens almost everywhere we go. More than ever, our world is becoming one big canvas of sophisticated, high-resolution images – a modern collection of visual stories.

Digital screens are on our computers and play stations and in headsets or helmets with screens inside. They show us a virtual reality, a 3D world that allows us to interact with it. Digital screens are on our wrists; they're in our hands on smartphones and tablets; they're in shopping centres selling products; they're in cars and aeroplane seats; they're in photo frames and even on our fridges at home.

Screens are everywhere, and most are connected to 'the cloud'. We can control the stories we see on our screens with our fingertips, with our voices or with gestures. What's more, screens are becoming an extension of ourselves, a part of our own personal story. Screens tell us our heart rates, our stress levels, our exercise levels and what we're eating. Companies can even identify what we like and then make certain information or products appear on our screens when we shop on the Internet.

We can take 360-degree images with a smartphone. Social network sites have introduced the possibility of allowing 360-degree videos. These videos allow our friends and fans to see the scenes and stories happening all around us. We can already experience smells and movement in 4D cinemas. Soon 360-degree cinemas will be an experience, too. Audiences will feel like they're right in the middle of a scene, watching the action taking place around them. As Shakespeare said, 'All the world's a stage.' Now that stage is on a screen!

2 Read and answer the questions.

1. What were the first 'screens' ever used?

____

2. How are modern images different from images from the past?

____

3. What digital screen can you wear on your body?

____

4. What types of information can a screen tell us about ourselves?

____

5. How can we tell our friends stories about ourselves?

____

6. Why do you think the stories are more about how we see things through technology rather than what we see?

____

3 **List five different places we find screens.** Write notes for each and describe one way we use that screen.

Screen	Use

4 **Write questions.** Find out how your friends or classmates use their screens.

____

____

____

____

GRAMMAR

Reported speech: Describing what others say

She says, 'I can't draw!'	She says (that) she can't draw.
He said, 'I think I will join an art class.'	He said he would join an art class.
'Put the tops on my pens.'	The illustrator tells/is telling/told them to put the tops on his pens.
'Will you help me?' she asked.	She asked (me) if I would help her.

We use reported speech to tell someone else what another person said. (This is different from direct or quoted speech when we quote the speaker's exact words between quotation marks.)

When the reporting verb – *say, tell, ask* – is in the present, there is no tense change to the verb. When the reporting verb is in the past – *said, told, asked* – the verb tenses change as follows:

present → past *will, can* → *would, could*

Remember to change the pronouns in the reported speech to represent the speaker's point of view. She said, '*My friend likes landscape paintings.' She said* **her friend** *liked landscape paintings.*

To report a command, use *told* + person + the infinitive with *to.*

1 **Listen.** Which picture do the speakers talk about? Write A, B or C. Then report what they said. Complete the sentences. Remember to change the pronoun where necessary. 034

A. 

B. 

C. 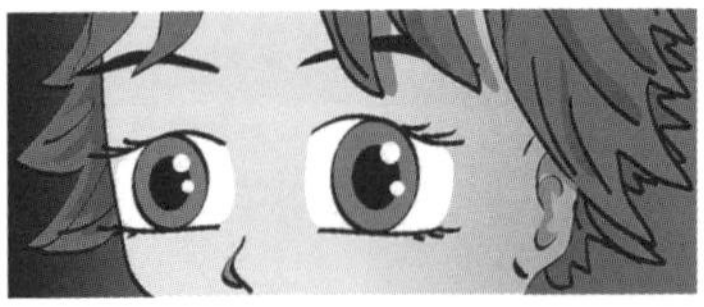

_____ 1. She said _______________________________.

_____ 2. He says the subject _______________________________.

_____ 3. She said _______________________________.

_____ 4. She said _______________________________.

_____ 5. He asked _______________________________.

_____ 6. He told me _______________________________.

_____ 7. She asked _______________________________.

2 **Read Sol's message to his friend.** Underline the reported speech. Write the actual words people say.

Hi Esme,

I'm looking for ideas for my end-of-year art project. <u>The teacher told us to take a photo of the town that would tell a story</u>. My mum laughed and said that was impossible because the town was so modern! My dad told me to take a photo of the river. He said that before people built roads, they travelled on the river. My uncle says that you can see parts of an old bridge over the river. Serge told me to forget the old stuff and take photos of the modern shopping centre. My grandma says that my grandad was a shipbuilder, so I should visit the port.

I think my sister had the best idea. She asked me if there was one thing that visually represented the town. I couldn't think of one. So she told me to take a lot of photos of the town and use a method called *collage*!

What do you think? Let me know.

Thanks,

Sol

1. The teacher said, 'Take a photo of the town that will tell a story.'
2. My mum said, ______
3. My dad said, ______
4. He said, ______
5. My uncle says, ______
6. Serge said, ______
7. Grandma says, ______
8. My sister asked, ______
9. She said, ______

WRITING

We use reported speech and quoted speech (when we use quotation marks to surround the exact words a person said) to make what somebody says part of our story. In reported speech, changes of pronoun and tense may be necessary.

As he left, he said, 'I'll be back.'
As he left, he said that he would be back.

'Sit down and have a slice of cake,' my aunt tells me each time I visit.
My aunt tells me to sit down and have a slice of cake each time I visit.

'Do you really like climbing?' my dad asked when I showed him the photo.
My dad asked if I really liked climbing when I showed him the photo.

1 Organise.

1. Your task is to choose a photo of a friend or family member and write the story that the photo tells. Try to remember conversations you had when the photo was taken. Include reported speech and quotations. On the lines below, write some of what was said.

____

____

____

____

2. Plan your writing. You'll need an introductory paragraph with a topic sentence. Your topic sentence will explain why you chose this particular photo. Write your topic sentence here.

____

   You'll need two to three body paragraphs. Describe the context in which the photo was taken, why it was a memorable occasion and what people said, asked or told you.

   Finally, you'll need a short concluding paragraph. Try to summarise what effect the person in the photo and the place or moment has had on your life.

2 Write.

1. Go to page 123 in your book. Re-read the model and writing prompt.
2. Write your first draft. Check for organisation, content, punctuation, capitalisation and spelling.
3. Write your final draft. Share it with your teacher and classmates.

Now I can ...

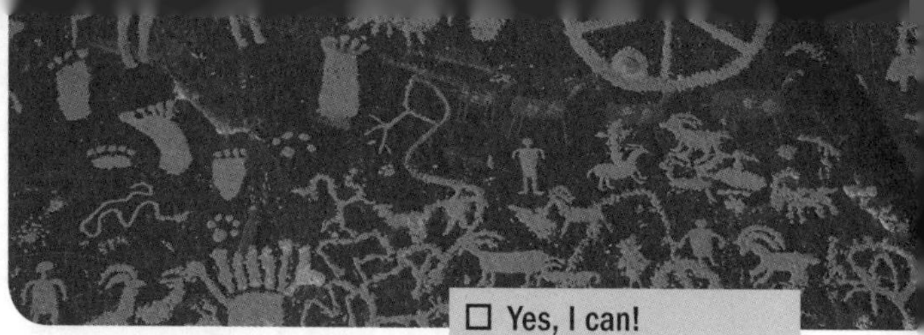

· talk about images to tell important stories.

☐ Yes, I can!
☐ I think I can.
☐ I need more practice.

'A picture can paint a thousand words.' Do you agree? Why or why not?

____

____

____

· use the past passive to describe past actions and processes.

☐ Yes, I can!
☐ I think I can.
☐ I need more practice.

Rewrite the sentences using the past passive.

1. The magic lantern used candles to create a moving image.

   ____

2. Thomas Edison invented a machine to watch cartoons.

   ____

3. Robert Capa took meaningful pictures of the Spanish Civil War.

   ____

· use reported speech to describe what others said.

☐ Yes, I can!
☐ I think I can.
☐ I need more practice.

1. What did a friend say or ask you yesterday?

   ____

2. What did a teacher or parent tell you to do last week?

   ____

· write a narrative essay about the story that a photo tells.

☐ Yes, I can!
☐ I think I can.
☐ I need more practice.

If you could choose one photo to frame tomorrow, which one would it be? Why? Remember a conversation connected to the photo.

____

____

____

YOU DECIDE Choose an activity. Go to page 96.

Unit 8

Perform and Create

1 **In each group, cross out the word that doesn't belong.** Write a reason. Then read each definition and write the word. Who is the famous composer?

1.	lyrics	~~composer~~	beats	fame
2.	composer	performer	lyrics	disc jockey
3.	influential	vary	manipulate	expose
4.	entertainment	recognition	self-expression	performer
5.	satisfaction	beats	manipulation	recognition

1. 'Composer' refers to a person, the others refer to things.
2. ______________________________
3. ______________________________
4. ______________________________
5. ______________________________

1. A person who entertains by singing or acting ___ ___ ___ ___ ___ ___ ___ ___ ___
2. To cause people to experience something ___ ___ ___ ___ ___ ___
3. To be or make something different ___ ___ ___ ___
4. The words to a song ___ ___ ___ ___ ___ ___
5. Having the power to cause changes ___ ___ ___ ___ ___ ___ ___ ___ ___ ___ ___

The composer is ___ ___ Z ___ ___ ___.

2 **Match the statement halves.** Write the letter.

_____ 1. Composers only write music

_____ 2. Music isn't only enjoyment;

_____ 3. Once some DJs gain fame and recognition,

_____ 4. When you see a symphony orchestra play together,

_____ 5. Applause is the only indication

_____ 6. Children should be exposed to music

_____ 7. Anyone can manipulate music

a. with just a smartphone.

b. from birth.

c. their music is no longer interesting.

d. that the audience is satisfied with the entertainment.

e. it can be influential in the way we think.

f. as a form of self-expression.

g. you realise teamwork between performers is essential.

3 **Listen.** Does the speaker agree or disagree with the statements? Tick *Agree* (A) or *Disagree* (D). 035

	A	D
1.	☐	☐
2.	☐	☐
3.	☐	☐
4.	☐	☐

	A	D
5.	☐	☐
6.	☐	☐
7.	☐	☐

4 **Listen again.** Write your own response for each statement you hear. 036

1. ______________________________

2. ______________________________

3. ______________________________

4. ______________________________

5. ______________________________

6. ______________________________

7. ______________________________

GRAMMAR

Gerunds and infinitives

Learning music is important. (subject)

I like **listening** to pop music. (object)

I'm interested **in learning** about jazz. (object of preposition)

I love **seeing / to see** live performances.

It's sad **to miss** their performance.

I turned up the volume **to listen** to the lyrics.

A *gerund* is a verb that acts like a noun. It can be used where nouns are used. Some verbs, such as *like* and *hate*, can be followed by gerunds and/or infinitives with *to*. The *infinitive* with *to* can follow adjectives such as *sad*, *happy* and *important*. The infinitive can also be used to express purpose and why we do/did something.

1 **Read.** Circle the correct answers. (Sometimes both answers are possible.)

1. Some people only like **listening / to listen** to one type of music. I think it's good **varying / to vary**.
2. **Co-ordinating / To co-ordinate** dance movements in a ballet must be very difficult.
3. I'm bored with **hearing / to hear** the same beats over and over again.
4. He used his fame and music **informing / to inform** others about climate change.
5. It's essential **buying / to buy** tickets early **seeing / to see** the band's performance.
6. My friend hates **dancing / to dance** to hip-hop music.
7. I'm interested in **adding / to add** electronic effects to my music.
8. I prefer **playing / to play** an instrument. **Dancing / To dance** is too tiring!
9. What do you think about **to listen / listening** to folk music?
10. We forgot **buying / to buy** tickets for tonight's concert.

2 **Listen to the radio programme.** Answer the questions in full sentences. 037

1. Who writes Taylor Swift's lyrics?

____

2. Why did her parents move to Nashville when Taylor was young?

____

____

3. What are some reasons young people love listening to her songs?

____

____

4. Who was excited about Taylor's talent? Why?

____

5. What's one reason Taylor may have stopped playing her guitar in public?

____

____

6. What indications were there of the success of her first pop album?

____

7. Why did she open the Taylor Swift Education Center?

____

____

____

3 **Read the answers.** Write the questions. Then answer the same question about yourself.

1. I prefer to listen to mixes by my favourite DJs when I'm on my own.

____

(You) ____

2. I get bored with listening to folk music.

____

(You) ____

3. I'm excited about starting dance rehearsals with a professional choreographer!

____

(You) ____

1 **Listen and read.** As you read, think about what conclusions you can draw about the importance of music. 038

The Sound of Glue

A In front of huge stages where singers, bands and orchestras perform, people do things together: they sing, wave their arms in the air, hold hands and dance. Thousands of people attend music performances and melt into one big co-ordinated group. They become one big group member.

B Researchers have theories about this. Many believe that music is a type of social glue. If you think of concerts, military music, music played at sporting events and national anthems, they all seem to unite us through emotions. Music is influential in the way people feel and behave all together at once.

C Researchers tell us that as humans, our main motivation in life is to be good group members. They believe that some people feel best when they lose their individual identities. Even when we listen to music on our own, we're connecting to others through the rhythms, beats or lyrics we hear and the thoughts they bring.

D Researchers believe that music brought and kept early humans close together thousands of years ago. Even before the earliest musical instruments and the invention of language, our ancestors probably used music to communicate. Researchers suggest that sound and music were the 'glue' for the first human societies and were very important in helping early modern humans create a sense of group identity and trust. This was important for successful living, hunting and migrating.

E The first music was probably just sounds. As we know, even music without lyrics can make us feel happy or sad. The tone of a voice can tell us how someone is feeling emotionally. It's possible that music and language both evolved because early humans needed to communicate their emotions to others in a group. As groups became larger, humans needed to find better and more efficient ways to express themselves.

F Of course, the first sounds were not that musical! They were probably more like grunts than the pure sound of an opera singer! What seems to be clear is that music brought people together thousands of years ago and it still does.

2 **Match each summary with a paragraph.** Write the letter.

_____ 1. It's human nature to want to be part of a group.

_____ 2. Music has a strong influence on us.

_____ 3. Sounds have changed, but the purpose is still the same.

_____ 4. Communicating emotions became important.

__A__ 5. In concerts, we become one.

_____ 6. For early humans, music helped to give a group identity.

3 **Make a list of the researchers' conclusions from the article.** Do you agree that music is like 'glue'? Give your reasons.

Conclusions

4 **Answer the questions and explain your own experience about being in a group.**

1. How do you feel when you listen to music in a group?

____

____

____

2. What difference do you find between listening to music in a group and listening to it on your own?

____

____

____

GRAMMAR

Sense verbs + infinitive: Describing what you see, hear and feel

I **saw** *the lights* **flash** with the beat of the music.
Can you **hear** *the ice* **break** in parts of their song?
It's strange to **feel** *the floor* **move** when everybody dances!
We **watched** *the couple* **dance** the tango.
We **had watched** *the flash mob* **come** together.

When we use sense verbs, we follow this structure: sense verb + object + infinitive (without *to*).

1 **Complete each sentence with a verb from the box.**

come on	open	pick up	read	start	walk

1. I felt my mouth ____________ as I picked up the microphone to sing!
2. I saw the lights ____________ behind me on the stage.
3. I heard the audience ____________ to applaud.
4. I watched the band ____________ onto the stage and ____________ their instruments.

2 **Listen.** Answer the questions. Use a sense verb and an infinitive in each answer. 039

1. What did the writer hear?

____

2. What things did he see become saxophones?

____

3. What did he see dustbins and X-rays transform into?

____

4. How did he feel about the way the instruments played?

____

5. What has he watched?

____

3 **Read the poem.** Underline the sense verbs and infinitives. Then use the sentence starters to write your own poem. Make sure you use the infinitive form.

This week we had to write about what we hear, see and feel. We didn't have to write a poem, but that's what I wanted to do. I thought I would upload it to see what you all think.

Mixed Emotions

When I see masterpieces on a wall before me,
I feel how the past and the present connect.
When I hear violins soar like clouds in the sky,
I feel my heart soar, too.
When I hear ice crack and break,
I know what a fragile world we live in.
When I see plastic float on rivers to the sea,
I am sad for the living things in the way.
When I feel the sun shine on my face,
I remember our place in the universe.
When I watch a small child take its first steps,
I am excited about what the future will bring.
Life is a symphony of sights, sounds and feelings.

When I see ______________________________,
______________________________.

When I hear ______________________________,
______________________________.

When I hear ______________________________,
______________________________.

When I see ______________________________,
______________________________.

When I feel ______________________________,
______________________________.

When I watch ______________________________,
______________________________.

WRITING

In an explanatory essay, we teach our reader about a topic. We don't include our opinion. In the first paragraph, we should identify the topic we're going to write about. Then, we provide additional facts, details and examples to help the reader understand the topic better.

1 Organise.

1. Your task is to write an essay to explain a type of artistic expression. Look through your book for examples of artistic expression and then choose a type you're interested in. Remember that artistic expression can include painting, sculpting, writing, composing and performing. Choose your topic and then research facts, details and examples. Make notes about what you want your reader to know about your topic.

Form of artistic expression:	
Facts	**Details and examples**
______________________	______________________
______________________	______________________
______________________	______________________
______________________	______________________
______________________	______________________

2. Plan your writing. You'll need an introductory paragraph with a topic sentence to introduce the form of artistic expression you're going to explain. Think about a topic sentence that will draw your audience in.

   ____

   You'll need two or three body paragraphs. Think about what aspect of artistic expression you're going to describe in each paragraph. Support it with interesting and unusual facts and details.

   Finally, you'll need to finish with a general statement that concludes your explanation. Remember *not* to give your own opinion.

2 Write.

1. Go to page 139 in your book. Re-read the model and writing prompt.
2. Write your first draft. Check for organisation, content, punctuation, capitalisation and spelling.
3. Write your final draft. Share it with your teacher and classmates.

Now I can ...

- **talk about music and performing arts.**

  ☐ Yes, I can!
  ☐ I think I can.
  ☐ I need more practice.

  What music or performing art appeals to you the most? Give reasons.

  ____

  Why do you think we listen to music? ______________________________

  ____

- **use gerunds and infinitives.**

  ☐ Yes, I can!
  ☐ I think I can.
  ☐ I need more practice.

  Write four sentences using a gerund or infinitive. Use the clues.

  1. (as a subject) ______________________________
  2. (as an object) ______________________________
  3. (as an object of a preposition) ______________________________
  4. (to express purpose) ______________________________

- **use sense verbs + infinitive to describe what you see, hear and feel.**

  ☐ Yes, I can!
  ☐ I think I can.
  ☐ I need more practice.

  Choose an appropriate sense verb and finish each sentence.

  1. Sometimes, my family __________ me sing when ______________________.
  2. If I __________ my favourite singer walk towards me, ______________________.
  3. I __________ the floor move when ______________________.

- **write an explanatory essay about a type of artistic expression.**

  ☐ Yes, I can!
  ☐ I think I can.
  ☐ I need more practice.

  Explain one way you express or would like to express yourself artistically. Use facts and examples.

  ____

  ____

  ____

  ____

  ____

  ____

  ____

YOU DECIDE **Choose an activity.** Go to page 96.

Units 7–8 Review

1 **Read.** Fill in each blank with a word from the box.

abstract	**canvas**	**images**	**masterpieces**	**meaningful**
method	**permanent**	**represents**	**scene**	**shocking**
sophisticated	**symphony**	**traditional**	**understanding**	**visual**

The Sounds of Visual Stories

Neil Harbisson is an artist who can't see colour. However, thanks to a special device, he now has an (1) ________________ of what colour could look like. He wears a (2) ________________ device that changes all the colours in a (3) ________________ into sound waves so that each colour (4) ________________ a musical note. This means he can hear a (5) ________________ of colour instead of seeing everything in greys. He feels that this (6) ________________ of hearing colour has made him into a human robot because the device has become a (7) ________________ part of him and his senses.

When he goes to an art gallery, Neil listens to the (8) ________________ of famous artists and understands the colours of the (9) ________________. At first, he found it (10) ________________ because everything was so noisy.

Later, Neil started to paint sound portraits by changing the sounds into colour on a (11) ________________. His subjects may be a piece of music, a speech by a famous person or an everyday object. The results are bright, (12) ________________ paintings of colourful rectangles. In this way, Neil creates a (13) ________________ story through the sounds that are so (14) ________________ to him.

2 **Listen.** Underline each correct answer. 040

1. The group first started as *animal trainers / street performers.*
2. The name Cirque du Soleil is a tribute to *Quebec / the Sun.*
3. The performers are from *many different countries / Canada.*
4. Costume designers and composers *play an essential part / are robotic.*
5. Each show *has 1,300 performers / is very visual.*
6. Their audiences *prefer realistic performances / are exposed to imaginary worlds.*

3 **Complete the sentences.** Use the *gerund* or *infinitive* of the words in brackets.

1. I can feel my voice ______________________ (become) quieter as I walk into a theatre.
2. It's essential for a musician ______________________ (practise) music every day.
3. In rehearsal, I watched ballet dancers ______________________ (work) with the choreographer. I was amazed!
4. She ran back ______________________ (get) her camera.
5. The teens were excited about ______________________ (form) a folk dancing group.
6. ______________________ (create) animations for TV has various stages.
7. We heard the symphony orchestra ______________________ (start) to play.

4 **Write.** Change each sentence so that the meaning is the same. Use reported speech for 1–4 and the past passive for 5–8.

1. 'Music makes the brain work better.'

   The researcher says ____.
2. 'There's a lot of new research on exposing children to music.'

   She told me ____.
3. 'Musical training can keep your brain sharp.'

   They said ____.
4. 'Will you play an instrument at school?'

   My friend asked me ____.
5. Early people made primitive instruments from tree trunks and animal skins.

   Instruments ____.
6. They exposed the audience to an amazing light show.

   The audience ____.
7. A computer designed the costumes for their performance.

   The costumes for their performance ______________________________.
8. They used recycled material to make the instruments.

   Recycled materials ____.

YOU DECIDE Choose an activity. Unit 1

☐ **1** Brainstorm as many different jobs as you can in one minute. Then, with a classmate, discuss the different skills and qualities you would need for each job. Which job would you be the best at? Explain why. Use as many words from the box as possible.

co-operative	**determined**	**energetic**
enthusiastic	**generous**	**helpful**
open-minded	**outgoing**	**patient**
responsible	**self-confident**	

☐ **2** Use question tags to make statements about the following topics.

Life as an only child
Life as a teenager
Being competitive
Following a recipe
Fast food

Example: *I'm an only child. That doesn't mean I'm spoilt, does it?*

☐ **3** Respond to each sentence with the special use of *it*.

I did really well in my exam!
I need to get up!
My bananas are all soft!
The journey takes six hours by car!
The sun is out!

☐ **4** **Work in pairs.** It's your birthday. With your best friend, make plans about the different things you can do to celebrate. Decide exactly what you will do. Then discuss.

- Assign roles.
- Practise the conversation.
- Act out the conversation in class, or use a phone or tablet to make a video.

☐ **5** **Write.** Choose two superheroes. Write about the ways they are similar and different. Explain which of the two is your favourite and why.

- To plan your writing, follow the steps on page 10 of your workbook.
- Share your writing with your teacher and classmates.

☐ **6** You saw this announcement in a local newspaper.

A part-time babysitter is needed for a friendly family in the city. We have two boys, ages 5 and 8. Experience with children is essential. Duties include preparing lunch and taking children outside to play.

Write to the family explaining your experience and why you would be a good candidate for the job. Ask questions about your hours of work and additional duties.

Write approximately 150 words.

YOU DECIDE Choose an activity.

1 If you had to choose any animal as a pet, which would you choose? Give your reasons. Compare your choice of pet with a classmate's. Use the following words to help you.

aggressive	**filthy**	**poisonous**
bite	**hurt**	**unpopular**
destroy	**misunderstood**	**untrue**
disgusting	**myth**	**upset**
fangs	**pest**	**venom**

2 Read the statements. Use the following four expressions to speculate on each situation in the past: *could have, might have, may have* and *must have*.

- The girl was shaking.
- The farmer was angry.
- The family didn't answer when he knocked on the door.

3 Answer the questions in full sentences. Notice if the verbs are followed by infinitives with or without *to*.

- What did you help somebody do recently?
- What things don't your parents let you do at home?
- What chores do your parents ask you to do?
- What do you plan to do next weekend?

4 **Work in pairs.** You want a pet snake. Your mum and dad are against this idea.

Role-play the dialogue between you and one of your parents. Come to a final decision.

- Assign roles.
- Think about the arguments for and against having a pet snake.
- Practise the dialogue.
- Act out the dialogue in class, or use a phone or tablet to make a video.

5 **Write.** You have asked a friend to look after your pet rat while you are on holiday. Describe how he/she must look after your pet every day. Make sure you explain what kind of exercise it needs and what to do if it becomes aggressive.

- Research how to look after rats.
- To plan your writing, follow the steps on page 20 in your workbook.
- Share your writing with your teacher and classmates.

6 Your pet tarantula has escaped! Write a flyer to hand out to neighbours and to put in shop windows. Describe the tarantula and its behaviour so that people are not scared and know what to do when they find it.

Use no more than 100 words to write your flyer.

YOU DECIDE Choose an activity. Unit 3

☐ **1** Do you prefer working in a group in class or working on your own? What are the advantages and disadvantages of each? Does your classmate share the same ideas as you? Try to include at least four of the following words in your conversation.

assume	**co-ordinated**	**leader**
belong to	**efficient**	**realised**
consensus		

☐ **2** Write each of the following 12 verbs on a strip of paper. Shuffle the strips and place them face down on a table. Turn the strips over one at a time and race your partner to write a sentence using the verb.

be associated with	**point out**
come across	**respond to**
deal with	**talk over**
work out	**think about**
go through	**turn out**
look at	**wonder about**

☐ **3** You are part of a group that wants to make changes to improve your town. To get ready for your meeting, rewrite your notes. Use (*not*) *enough*, *too much* and *too many*. Add some more ideas to the list.

- Cars in the town centre
- Need more trees and plants
- Only one sports facility
- Dance clubs are noisy and neighbours can't sleep.
- Dog owners want more green spaces to walk their dogs.

☐ **4** **Work in pairs.** You and your partner have just watched a documentary on animal group behaviour. Choose an animal group. Talk about what amazed you about the animals and how group behaviour helps these animals survive.

flock of birds	**school of fish**
herd of elephants	**swarm of ants**
pack of wolves	

- Take notes on the two groups of animals.
- Practise the conversation.
- Act out the conversation in class, or use a phone or tablet to make a video.

☐ **5** **Write.** Prepare a speech to give to parents whose children are new at your school. Explain why playing a team sport is the best way for students to learn to work together. Give examples of how team sports can be beneficial.

- To plan your writing, follow the steps on page 32 in your workbook.
- Share your writing with your teacher and classmates.

☐ **6** A friend has written to you asking for advice.

From: Joe To: Gloria
Subject: My sister's party

Help! My little sister is going to have her 8th birthday party at home. My mum has asked me to help out with the entertainment. Have you got any ideas for fun group activities I can do with the children? Thank you!

Write to your friend with your ideas. Use no more than 100 words.

YOU DECIDE Choose an activity.

☐ **1** Describe a piece of clothing you see someone wearing without saying what it is. Use at least five words from the list below. Ask a classmate to guess!

attractive	**leather**	**style**
designer	**material**	**synthetic**
eco-friendly	**popular**	**trendy**
fashion		

☐ **2** Read the steps to dye a T-shirt using a natural dye.

How to dye a T-shirt using beetroot!

1. Wash the T-shirt.
2. Cut the beetroot, put it in water in a pot and simmer for an hour.
3. Remove the beetroot, put the T-shirt in the red liquid and simmer for one hour.
4. Rinse very well and dry.

Always wash with dark clothes … unless you want some red on all your clothes!

Describe the process using the passive voice.

☐ **3** You received this text message from a friend.

My mum says I spent too much money during the summer and I can't buy new clothes for the next three months. ☹ What do I do now? I need to get something cool for the school party!!

Respond with three short text messages. Comment on your friend's problem using *could*, *should*, *could have* or *should have*.

☐ **4** **Work in pairs.** Interview a young designer.

- Research a young designer.
- Prepare five questions.
- Assign the roles of interviewer and designer.
- Practise the interview.
- Act out the interview in class, or use a phone or tablet to make a video.

☐ **5** **Write.** Persuade your readers to wear or not to wear a certain type of clothing. Support your point of view with facts and statistics.

- To plan your writing, follow the steps on page 42 in your workbook.
- Share your writing with your teacher and classmates.

☐ **6** This is part of an e-mail you received from a friend in the United States.

For my homework project I have to write about what children my age in another country like to wear these days. What's the latest fashion where you live? Do you and your friends like it? Why?

Respond to the e-mail. Write at least 100 words.

YOU DECIDE Choose an activity. Unit 5

☐ **1** If you were an animal that could fly, which animal would you be? Why? Explain your reasons to a partner. How are your animals similar and different? Use the following words to help you.

adaptation	**glide**	**skilled**
allow	**hollow**	**support**
capability	**land**	**take off**
evolve	**limited**	**weight**
flight	**powered**	

☐ **2** Your friend, who is studying English, isn't sure how to use the past and past perfect tenses to distinguish the first of two actions. Can you help your friend?

I _____ (to be) very scared the first time I _____ (to fly) in an aeroplane when I _____ (to be) four. I _____ (to scream) for an hour before a flight attendant _____ (to give) me a toy! Apparently, all the passengers _____ (to complain). But amazingly, last year I _____ (to learn) to paraglide. My mum can't believe it!

☐ **3** Look at the time line of Ana's activities. What had she been doing the hour before?

Watch a documentary
6 p.m.
Write an essay on the history of flight
7 p.m.
Eat dinner
8 p.m.
Message friends
9 p.m.
Read in bed
10 p.m.
Go to sleep

Example: *Before 6 p.m., Ana had been watching a documentary. Before 7 p.m., ...*

☐ **4** **Work in pairs.** Read the following statement.

A jet pack will be the best way to travel in the future.

Do you agree or disagree with this statement? Give your reasons. Make notes about what you and your partner will discuss.

- Practise your dialogue.
- Act out the dialogue in class, or use a phone or tablet to make a video.

☐ **5** **Write.** Write a classification essay to describe the different flying experiences of hang gliding, skydiving and using a jet pack.

- To plan your writing, follow the steps on page 54 in your workbook.
- Share your writing with your teacher and classmates.

☐ **6** Your family wants to plan something special for your mum and dad's wedding anniversary. In a travel magazine, you see this advertisement for helicopter rides.

From the moment you take off, you will feel the excitement of soaring above this amazing waterfall. Come and experience the flight of a lifetime!

Write to the company. Find out more information and ask questions about the helicopter ride.

Write at least 100 words.

YOU DECIDE Choose an activity. Unit 6

☐ **1** If you could choose, which place would you explore: space or the depths of the ocean? Talk to a classmate who wants to explore a different place to you. Share reasons for your choices. Use the following words to help you.

aspects	**fundamental**	**proof**
chance	**instruments**	**vast**
detect	**lead to**	

☐ **2** Use present and past conditionals to answer the question about the following situation.

What would you have done if planet Earth had been invaded by visitors from other planets?

☐ **3** Write a report to compare how these sets of devices have been working. Use the following adverbs: *fast, accurately, efficiently, precisely.*

Printer X / Printer Y

Smartphone camera / Tablet camera

Mars Rover I / Mars Rover II

Quadcopter D5 / Quadcopter D10

☐ **4** **Work in pairs.** Interview the first astronaut to travel to Mars.

- Re-read information about Mars.
- Prepare five questions.
- Assign the roles of astronaut and interviewer.
- Practise the interview.
- Act out the interview in class, or use a phone or tablet to make a video.

☐ **5** **Write.** Write about the argument that it's better to focus on looking after our own planet than to send missions to other worlds.

- To plan your writing, follow the steps on page 64 of your workbook.
- Share your writing with your teacher and classmates.

☐ **6** Imagine that you're an astronaut on the International Space Station. You are keeping a blog of what your life is like there. Write today's blog.

Write at least 100 words.

YOU DECIDE Choose an activity. Units 7–8

☐ **1** Observe a painter painting. Write about the process in the past passive.

The painter drew an outline of the subject.
She mixed the colours.
She applied the paint to the canvas.
She cleaned her brushes.
She left the portrait to dry.

☐ **2** Rewrite the sentences in reported speech. Indicate who is speaking.

'You can't take photos inside the gallery.'
'Stand in the light to the left of the tree.'
'Can you take my photo next to the statue?'

Use *say*, *tell* and *ask*.

☐ **3** **Write.** Observe a group of people in your town, outside your window or at school. Invent a story about what the scene tells you. Use reported speech and quotations to tell what you think people are saying.

- To plan your writing, follow the steps on page 76 in your workbook.
- Share your writing with your teacher and classmates.

☐ **4** You see this announcement for new after-school clubs in your school magazine.

New Clubs Wanted After School
Table tennis, guitar playing and cooking have been suggested. Make a suggestion and we will publish your article in next month's magazine.

Make a suggestion for an art and photography club. Explain why it would be a good idea. Write about 100 words.

☐ **1** Imagine that you are going to interview your favourite musical artist for a local cultural magazine. Use each of the expressions in the box to form your questions before the interview.

bored with	**excited about**	**like/love/hate**
difficult to	**important to**	**prefer**

☐ **2** You have just given your first performance in front of the whole school. Write down your impressions about the experience. Use the sentence starters below and an infinitive.

I saw ...	*I watched ...*
I heard ...	*I felt ...*

☐ **3** **Write.** Choose a topic that you are passionate about that isn't related to music. Share your passion by writing an explanatory essay that includes facts, details and examples to help others understand the topic.

- To plan your writing, follow the steps on page 86 in your workbook.
- Share your writing with your teacher and classmates.

☐ **4** Your friend has sent you this e-mail.

From: Darrah To: Sofia
Subject: Summer concert

Hi! I have just seen that there will be a big summer festival near where I live. There will be some great artists and DJs playing. I wondered if you'd like to come and go to a few outdoor concerts with me?

What do you think? Let me know and I'll buy tickets.

Write your answer in about 100 words.